THE FUTURES

THE
FUTURES

THE **Rise** OF THE **Speculator**

AND THE **Origins** OF THE

World's Biggest Markets

EMILY LAMBERT

BASIC BOOKS
A Member of the Perseus Books Group
New York

Copyright © 2011 by Emily Lambert

Published by Basic Books,
A Member of the Perseus Books Group

All rights reserved. Printed in the United States of America.
No part of this book may be reproduced in any manner whatsoever
without written permission except in the case of brief quotations
embodied in critical articles and reviews. For information, address
Basic Books, 387 Park Avenue South, New York, NY 10016-8810.

Books published by Basic Books are available at special discounts
for bulk purchases in the United States by corporations, institutions,
and other organizations. For more information, please contact
the Special Markets Department at the Perseus Books Group,
2300 Chestnut Street, Suite 200, Philadelphia, PA 19103,
or call (800) 810-4145, ext. 5000, or e-mail
special.markets@perseusbooks.com.

Designed by Brent Wilcox

Library of Congress Cataloging-in-Publication Data
Lambert, Emily, 1976-
   The futures : the rise of the speculator and the origins of the
world's biggest markets / Emily Lambert.—1st ed.
      p.   cm.
   Includes bibliographical references and index.
   ISBN 978-0-465-01843-7 (alk. paper)
   1. Chicago Mercantile Exchange.   2. Commodity exchanges—
Illinois—Chicago—History.   3. Chicago (Ill.)—History.   I. Title.
   HG6049.L36 2010
   332.64'40973—dc22

                                                        2010027676

10 9 8 7 6 5 4 3 2 1

To
Donato Joseph Colitto,
our little derivative.

CONTENTS

PROLOGUE
The Present

It is January 2010, and it is cold in Chicago. A man in a gray Chevrolet Impala drives into the city on Interstate 290. It's known locally as
the Eisenhower Expressway, or "the Eisenhower." Traffic reporters
often just call it "the Ike." He has driven the route a thousand times,
if not more. On the Eisenhower, an extension of Interstate 88, he
cuts through western suburbs that used to be farms. He passes
tough West Side neighborhoods, rail yards and warehouses, and
luxury condominiums on his way to the Loop, the area where the
elevated trains—Chicago's "L"—rattle in from the neighborhoods,
circle a section of the downtown area, and head back out again. As
he approaches, buildings jut up like glass and steel blades of prairie
grass. The old Sears Tower, recently renamed, looks particularly tall
from this angle, a black stripe against the morning sky.

The man, whose name is Charlie Andrews, is briefly in traffic but
not for long, which must be some kind of miracle in Chicago, where
there is always traffic. He prefers gray cars because the color hides
dirt as well as dirty snow. He navigates the Loop's many one-way
streets and stops short of Michigan Avenue, where tourists from
small farming towns sometimes walk down the street with mouths
agape and eyes wide as they wander between the skyscrapers. He
parks the Impala in a lot on the southern edge of the Loop.

Andrews walks to La Salle Street, the main artery of the financial district. He passes impressive, heavy buildings that block the
sunlight and cast long shadows. He's the kind of man you don't

necessarily notice, but if you do, you wonder whether he's lost or perhaps wandered in from a different place and decade. Andrews is seventy-two years old and six-foot-four, topped with a shock of white hair. He wears a green suit and an oval-shaped belt buckle, the kind you can find in glass cases at Alcala's Western Wear on West Chicago Avenue, an emporium popular with inhabitants of the city's many Latino neighborhoods. It's a rarity here on La Salle Street, where men wear blue suits, starched shirts, and the sort of shoes that benefit from frequent polishing.

Andrews enters a building at the end of the street that stops La Salle in its tracks, a Gotham-esque Art Deco tower at the end of the block. It looks taller than it really is. You might recognize it. It turns up in the background of movies. In *The Dark Knight*, a semi flips over in front of it. Today, in the snow, it looks like a giant armchair. An oversized clock ticks above the main entrance; on top of the building stands an aluminum statue, a few stories tall, of the goddess Ceres, the daughter of Saturn. Romans believed her to be the goddess of grains, or cereals. Here she's on lookout, or would be if her face had any features.

Andrews pushes through revolving doors into the lobby, which features nine kinds of marble and pillars meant to look like skyscrapers. Around him, woven into odd places like heating vents, are stylized decorative versions of wheat. Deeper into the building, the elevator doors close and reveal more sheaves of wheat, this time in a shape that resembles a martini glass. But this morning he doesn't get that far in.

The building's lobby features a newsstand, a bank, and a restaurant with large glass windows looking into the lobby. The restaurant, once called Sign of the Trader and now called Ceres, feels clubby and cliquey, the kind of place where men who know each other meet for hushed lunches. It would be full of smoke if this were the movies, or if Illinois hadn't banned smoking in public places. And it would be raucous and rowdy at the bar if the business being done upstairs in this building hadn't changed. That said, even now, every drink is a double.

Andrews enters the restaurant, takes a seat in a booth, and gives a waitress his order, a sole sandwich with tartar sauce. He gives the order slightly louder and slower than seems normal. But he is not from around here. He lives in Kanopolis, Kansas, population five hundred. His great-grandfather was a butcher from Scotland who moved to the States and shot buffalo to feed railroad crews. His grandfather bought a farm and cattle.

Cowboys are prone to some tall tales, and Andrews is no exception. He has a few stories, and he will tell most without hesitation. For example, while buying cattle he went to Mexico and met the actor John Wayne, with whom he went on a two-day bender. The rest of the story involves the phrase "fifteen fresh whores an hour." He left some to the imagination. There's another story, told by a friend of his who has an office upstairs, about a visit to Clayton, New Mexico. That's where that friend put a ranch horse in Andrews's hotel room as a prank. Andrews doesn't remember what provoked the prank, but he remembers the animal, as cowboys do. "I wanted that horse," he says, adding that he took it home. "He turned out to be a tremendous horse."

But the most interesting story Charlie Andrews tells has to do with the business he got into in Chicago. There he was, from Kansas, traveling to Mexico and around the United States, buying calves and light cattle on behalf of feedlots, which fattened them up to sell to slaughter. In El Paso in 1962, he opened a trading account with E. F. Hutton, a now-extinct brokerage company (best remembered for its ad tagline: "When E. F. Hutton talks, people listen"), and put $5,000 into it. He started trading something obscure—futures contracts on pork bellies. He became an active speculator. It fascinated him, he said, "because money is the way you keep score."

Shortly after he opened the account, Andrews went to Chicago, where millions of cattle were sold in its stockyards and killed in its packing plants. While there, he visited the building in the Loop where he sent his pork belly orders. It housed the Chicago Mercantile Exchange, a member-run club.

He continued to trade pork belly futures, and then futures contracts on cattle. As the stockyards declined, he got to know the futures traders better as their trade grew bright and exciting. Some were young and rambunctious like he was. In 1969 he saw a hog futures trader, happy after a good day, pour liquor on his chest and light it on fire for fun. Andrews spent many nights with them on stools at Division and State Streets, a then-lurid nightlife district that put him in close proximity with both mobsters and housing projects. One night he heard machine guns as he walked down an alley at 2:00 AM. He hid behind a Dumpster.

In 1973 he joined the small futures exchange. Some of the wildest things he saw, he saw there at what they called "the Merc." Men there were in the business of taking risks, and mostly with their own money. Some were successful. He saw a man rack up $10 million on a series of good trades. Many were not successful. He saw more than one trader on the floor lose everything. When new men came to trade, he learned to recognize the ones who wouldn't make it. He could predict who would take risks wildly, without considering the consequences, and who would eventually lose his money, confidence, and sense and be wheeled off the trading floor on a stretcher. Andrews stopped trading for himself early on, after he lost a large amount of money, but continued advising people.

The longer Andrews stayed, the more futures contracts he had to choose from. The traders branched out into foreign currencies, stocks, and interest rates. Five years after joining the Merc, the cowboy was a broker advising money managers in New York, Geneva, and other places. The work had an unfortunate side effect. Andrews left in 1995 for a two-year stint in jail after he pled guilty to one count of perjury in a case in which a customer of his was accused of running a Ponzi scheme. Andrews says that he was innocent but changed his testimony on the advice of his lawyer. He pled guilty, paid a $400,000 fine, and agreed to testify for the government only because he believed that he would not serve jail time. From prison, he successfully fought off civil suits and continued to call his office every day—collect—to relay his views on the market. When he was once again a free man, in 1997, he moved back to Chicago.

It felt different. The traders had long dominated their small corner of the financial world. But they were being overshadowed by a new group of faster, larger traders. Some traded with computers, others worked from offices with massive amounts of other people's money. While many were more sophisticated and educated, some of them started to remind Andrews of the traders who came to the trading floor and took risks with money they couldn't afford to lose, and inevitably did. The Merc members, to compete in the changing world, transformed their club into a public company and embraced technology. In 2005 Andrews moved back to Kansas to work from his home.

From there, he watched as prices in many markets skyrocketed. Food and oil prices shot up. So did home prices. But Andrews says he had learned in the cattle business and on the trading floor to sense when a market was frothy. In mid-2007, he says, he advised his customers in the financial markets to proceed with caution. He says a few did, while others ignored him and switched to different advisers.

In 2008 the markets crashed. That fall, the financial system ground to a near-dead halt. American taxpayers paid billions of dollars to prevent the financial system from collapsing. Andrews watched it on the news from his home office, with a view of his horses and pasture. When it happened, Andrews just shook his head and was amazed at how much had changed.

As Andrews talks, men walk by. Some wear colored trading jackets, and others wear suits. A man with graying hair sits at a table by the back wall, engrossed in conversation with an attractive female companion much younger than he. Another man, wearing a trading jacket, is hunched over his plate just a few tables away. Some are old enough to retire and play golf in Scottsdale or Naples. Instead, they are hanging around La Salle Street in the middle of the afternoon, in the dead of winter.

All of these men seem to know each other, and they tell a version of the same story. The details vary, mangled by time, whiskey, egos, and personal grudges. But it's about how their simple, overlooked business called futures grew into something far larger. They hang out here and cling to a clubhouse built when airmail was advanced technology. They're like the last guests at a party, tipsy, full of stories, and not quite sure how to get home.

PART I

Grain   +0.01

The place that became Chicago was founded on land known as Illinois Territory, named in a hat tip to the Native American groups that long inhabited the area. In 1808 the government built Fort Dearborn on a small hill above a river, near the shore of a large freshwater lake. The soldiers defended the fur trade. Chicago was built, literally, for trading.

By 1812 the people pushing into the western territory had annoyed and frightened the natives, who allied with the British to stop American expansion. On a hot summer morning that year, a few dozen men, women, and children evacuated the fort. They followed the lakefront and made it about a mile and a half south—to the area that would become Prairie Avenue, Millionaires' Row—where they were attacked by natives, who killed fifty-some people and lost some of their own in a matter of minutes. The surviving settlers surrendered. This was called the Fort Dearborn Massacre.

The attack scared off plenty of people, but the great national march westward was ultimately unstoppable. The army returned in 1816, and Illinois was admitted to the union two years later. Fur traders and military men gave way to a parade of farmers, merchants, and other entrepreneurs who built log cabins and sod houses on the prairie and farmed some of the richest soil on the planet. They fought off disease, bad weather, animals, bandits, and the other unpredictable elements of life on the fringe.

In the 1830s, they started digging a canal. The goal was for the Irish workers doing the labor to dig a ditch that would connect the

Chicago and Illinois Rivers, thus linking the Great Lakes to the Mississippi River and putting Chicago in a good position to become a hub. It could be a center for business to rival and maybe overtake other hopeful cities, like St. Louis.

The canal sparked a land rush. An Englishwoman traveling through town in the 1830s described streets crowded with land speculators and storekeepers hawking farms and lots. In 1835 a man named William B. Ogden arrived from New York to oversee his brother-in-law's 150-acre real estate investment. He sent back word that speculators were driving prices to ridiculous levels. Sure enough, it was a bubble, and land prices crashed in 1837.

Then came 1848, a year that a Chicago trader would describe 160 years later in his office with such fondness that it almost seemed like he had been there. That year the canal opened, the city's first railroad tracks were laid, and the telegraph arrived. Chicagoans stared excitedly into the future.

As Chicago became a hub, Ogden and eighty-two other men created a business organization that became the Chicago Board of Trade. At first the Board was just a group of businessmen. They met in a long, narrow room upstairs from a flour store at 101 South Water Street, on the south bank of the river, near where Fort Dearborn stood until 1857. Besides Ogden, there was Gurdon Hubbard, a Vermonter and future meatpacker and the city's first insurance man. There was John H. Kinzie, who was a son of one of the first settlers and who had seen and survived the Fort Dearborn Massacre. Some of these men had names destined for the Chicago street map. They got together to discuss and promote the city's commerce.

Before long, they started talking about grain, which was a big business in the frontier town. Some farmers hauled it in on rutted, muddy, bandit-ridden roads. But most were too busy taking care of their farms to make the trip. They sold their grain to local merchants, who brought it to Chicago by boat or railcar and then haggled in the streets. The Board of Trade decided that it made more sense to have one meeting place for everyone with grain to buy or sell and tried to lure them to their room on South Water Street, and to other rooms they rented around the area, eventually resorting to crackers, cheese, and ale.

Few showed up, but Chicago's weather gave them reason. The city was built roughly halfway between the North Pole and the Equator. Warm fronts from the south clashed with cold fronts from the north. As the seasons changed, temperatures swung from bitter cold winters to hot, humid summers. That's part of the funny story of this business, and one reason why it developed in Chicago instead of, say, Florida.

In late fall and winter, farmers growing corn along the river hauled it by oxcart and sled to the local grain merchant. The river and canal were sometimes already frozen, and merchants couldn't get the corn to Chicago, so they stored it in corn cribs during the winter. In the spring, the river thawed and sellers converged on Chicago and drove prices down to the point that it wasn't always worth making the trip. Farmers, traders liked to say later with theatrical flourish, would dump their corn in the river.

So river merchants started arranging to sell the corn in advance. Someone said, "Hey, I know it's cold and only March now, but I'll deliver three thousand bushels of corn to you next June for a penny cheaper than what you'd pay me today. Deal?" On March 13, 1851, three years after the Board of Trade was formed, two traders signed the first such timed contract—or at least the first one to make the textbook. A seller promised to deliver corn the following June for one cent per bushel less than the March price.

Similar contracts were traded at other places and times around the globe. Some traders point to the Bible, ancient Greece, medieval Europe, and seventeenth-century Japan to show they were following an established path. But this trade took root in Chicago in a way it hadn't before. People in the grain trade who were worried that prices would go up or down started trading these contracts. People who knew nothing about corn also started trading them. They saw an opportunity to make money by guessing the direction of corn prices, and they bought and sold the contracts before having to take or deliver corn. By the mid-1850s, a single contract could pass through several hands before finally ending up in the hands of a merchant who wanted corn. Around that time, traders finally started gathering in large numbers at the Board of Trade.

By 1856, the Board of Trade had several hundred members, and the trading room had grown crowded. The gypsylike exchange moved to the corner of South Water and La Salle Streets. In 1860 there were still more people who wanted to trade, so the Board moved again, to a new building built steps away at South Water and Wells Streets. The second story had a large hall, more than four thousand square feet, with frescoed walls and ceiling and uninterrupted views from one side of the room to the other. In that new space, they traded furiously because the demand for grain skyrocketed as northern and southern soldiers fought in civil war. The Union quartermaster, who was responsible for keeping the troops fed, ordered oats and pork in advance, and speculators dove in— those that didn't join the Board's own regiment. One of these traders, a man named Benjamin Hutchinson, made a small fortune in 1864. The next year, he must have heartily shaken hands with both General William Tecumseh Sherman and General Ulysses Grant when they visited the exchange.

It's hard to pinpoint the moment when the transformation occurred. But by 1865, the contracts started to look alike. Instead of buying and selling specific bags of grain, traders bought and sold grain that met a specific description—a certain grade of corn, for example. The contracts called for standardized grades of grain, to be delivered in standardized amounts, on standardized dates. With contracts that looked alike, it became easier to buy and sell them and to trade them like baseball cards. On October 13, 1865, two months after moving yet again to La Salle and Washington Streets, the Chicago Board of Trade adopted some rules for this trading. According to the late University of Illinois agriculture professor Thomas Hieronymus, who wrote a textbook on futures, that's the closest anyone can come to assigning a birth date to the modern futures contract.

If the forward contract was haute couture, the futures contract was strictly off-the-rack—a generic piece of paper. And the futures contract was a great equalizer. It attracted people like Hutchinson, who built a meatpacking plant in brand-new stockyards south of town. He didn't need much money to trade. With a small amount of money down, he could buy a futures contract and flip it for a large profit. As long as he bought low and sold higher, in either order, he would turn a profit.

The city was full of opportunity-seekers like him. It also had a bunch of thrill-seekers. Professional gamblers from Mississippi riverboats poured into Chicago and its gambling dens during the Civil War. Men bet on cards, checkers, horses, boxing, and rat fights. They filled neighborhoods like the Sands, just north of the river. A stretch of Randolph Street became known as Hair Trigger Block because so many men went there to settle their fights with guns.

With futures, traders were more than gamblers. Gamblers created risks to bet on. They threw dice that didn't have to be thrown. They ran horses that didn't have to run. But in the futures business, men had no need to manufacture risks because they bet on risks that would present themselves. The corn crop could fail. The farmers could be snowed in and unable to deliver grain. So the futures traders provided insurance. By locking in prices in advance, they took risks that other people didn't want. And the more the better. With traders milling around, whenever a farmer or merchant wanted to trade, someone was usually there at the Board of Trade to quote a price and make a deal. As traders, they quoted competitive prices and created smaller gaps between the buying and selling prices, shrinking what could be large swings in price.

Futures took off in Chicago because, in a sense, everyone there was speculating. Hopeful businessmen constructed warehouses, railroads, homes, and shops. Some built stockyards on swampland. When cholera broke out, they raised the city streets and reversed the flow of the river. Risk and opportunity were plentiful, and the futures contract concentrated much of that into a financial instrument. The people who traded futures became known as speculators.

The city itself briefly seemed like a losing bet. In October 1871, a fire broke out, and a story spread that a cow owned by Mrs. Catherine O'Leary kicked over a kerosene lamp and started the blaze. However it started, the fire burned down a quarter of the city and made close to 100,000 people homeless. It also burned the building that housed the Board of Trade. All the risks taken to that point—to move to Chicago, to put time and money into trains, canals, sewers, and grain elevators—seemed for naught. But some people in Chicago sized up the city and saw a clean, albeit smoking, slate. Contracts to rebuild were signed immediately. The Board of Trade moved into a temporary home while the Chamber of Commerce building that housed it was rebuilt. Chicago would come back taller than before—out of the fire and into the skyscraper.

The ancestors, as it were, of modern traders were not well liked. In 1878, R. K. Slosson, someone who was obviously fed up, wrote a letter to the publication *Western Rural*. He complained about the men at the Board of Trade. He said that they took advantage of farmers, and he said it in several descriptive ways. "They eulogize the doctrine that supply and demand fix the prices of grain," he wrote, then went on to call the Board members "liars," "unscrupulous gamblers," "bifurcated abominations in the sight of the Lord," "brotherhood banditti," and members of a "filching machine." "Like cannibal insects," he wrote, "they do not hesitate to eat each other up." Also, "they are banded together, and that too, under the eyes of the law, to rob farmers and country buyers, and their machinery is so simple and yet so perfect that success is theirs."

He had some legitimate gripes. Some early traders were particularly well behaved. Five firms owned the city's biggest grain elevators, which were huge storage warehouses that were like frontier skyscrapers. Some of the elevator men were Board of Trade members, and they worked creatively together to make money at the expense of farmers and merchants who paid to store grain. They fixed prices. They had railroads deliver grain to them, regardless of where it was supposed to go. The elevator owners spread rumors that grain was going bad so they could buy it for cheap. They bribed grain inspectors to disguise bad grain.

But slowly, over a few decades, the Board of Trade members, with some help from government officials, reined in the elevator men and pounded the business into shape. Quite literally, they pounded it into an octagon. Even though members gathered in one room to trade, they had trouble seeing each other. They pushed, shoved, and destroyed furniture while trying to buy and sell, and they fought in and around the building. So in 1870 a director suggested they use "raised steps," and that December the members introduced a circular platform that evolved into an octagonal series of steps. This was the pit, perhaps because it descended into the floor like one. Traders on the steps faced each other and looked into each other's eyes. They saw who was trading the most and who was buying or selling. They made deals in the open and established prices everyone could see.

They tracked the prices and displayed them on a quotation clock whose arms pointed to fractions of cents rather than minutes and hours. With that, a trader could see how much money he made or lost as easily as he could see if it was time for dinner. When the market closed, trades were tallied or "marked to market," and there were an equal number of winners and losers. Men whose futures positions had lost value paid money. The others collected it.

And with this, the futures market became a game. It became a speculative sport that captured headlines as the rich men of Chicago played it between their other business dealings and pursuits.

One of the finest players, it seemed, had predated the market by a few years. That was Joseph of *Amazing Technicolor Dreamcoat* fame in the Bible. Joseph advises the pharaoh of Egypt to store surplus grain. Then, when famine hits, people from all over, including his own brothers who'd sold him as a slave, come to Joseph. Thanks to dreams, he anticipated a shortage and profits from it.

Some of the Chicago traders—who met in the pit—also anticipated and profitted from shortages. They, however, used futures and stealth to create temporary, artificial shortages called "corners." Working alone or at times with others, a trader cornered a market by buying a controlling amount of something, often wheat. If he did it right, he ended up owning all the wheat in local elevators. When he bought, others sold, and those sellers promised to deliver wheat by a certain date. He knew that some sellers would grow and deliver the wheat while others, figuring that the price of wheat would fall, would plan to buy it for cheaper and deliver that. But when the time came, they wouldn't find any wheat to buy and deliver, in which case they were "cornered"—backed into a corner. To fulfill their obligations, they were forced to pay exorbitant prices to buy back futures contracts to cancel out their position. Sometimes they were forced to buy the contracts from the man who'd pulled off the corner at whatever price he demanded.

Because the shortage was artificial, the price hike was too. The man who cornered the futures market made a small bundle on futures. Then he sold the grain itself at a loss in a move that was called "burying the corpse." When he did that, the artificial shortage turned into a glut, and prices collapsed.

The first man to corner in a big way was Benjamin Hutchinson. An early fixture in the pit, "Old Hutch," as he was known, was a farm boy from Massachusetts who went into the shoe business and eventually made his way to Chicago, where a reporter described him as someone who had the "complexion of a liver sausage, and weighed only one hundred pounds." He went into the meatpacking business, then became a banker, lent money to men at the Board of Trade, and became a member of the Board.

Hutchinson was known as the king of the wheat pit. He had a throne—a wicker chair—on the trading floor. In 1881 it was estimated he was worth $10 million.

In 1888 Hutchinson led his most famous corner. He stealthily bought up wheat futures contracts. In the fall, a frost killed off a portion of the year's wheat crop. This worked to Hutchinson's advantage and made wheat even harder to get. On September 4, sellers wised up to his plotting, but there was little they could do. The market was going up (just like the world's first skyscraper, a brick structure a few blocks away). Showing off, Hutchinson had his broker buy 1 million bushels in a single trade. When the contract expired, sellers were indeed unable to find wheat to deliver. They were forced to buy back futures contracts directly from Hutchinson. He made millions on the deal, outraged local journalists, and embarrassed his son, who was then president of the Board. When the corner was over, the price of wheat crashed.

In the end, Old Hutch got some comeuppance. In 1891 he bought 3 million bushels of corn, due for delivery in July. But he didn't buy enough corn to successfully corner the market. The price dropped, and the futures contracts he had bought were worth less than he paid. He lost $2 million. His son settled his trading debts for him—and Old Hutch left for New York City. He rented a tiny office on Wall Street and slept in a swivel chair. In an article he wrote for the *North American Review*, he argued that there could never be another big, successful corner in wheat and compared the market to Niagara Falls, something men could influence but never truly control.

Hutchinson's actions made more of an impression than his writing. In 1897 a younger man, Joseph Leiter, tried to become the new wheat king. Leiter was born into money, the kind that paid for mansions, electric lights, live-in servants, and fashionable parties on Prairie Avenue. His father was a retailer in business with Marshall Field, who had a department store on State Street. The younger Leiter spent a year buying up 22 million bushels worth of wheat futures contracts and another 18 million bushels of actual wheat. He started when wheat was at seventy-three cents a bushel. It rose to a dollar, and then even higher.

He faced off against his father's neighbor, Philip Armour, one of Chicago's richest men. Armour had made his money in gold and then with a massive meat-packing operation by the stockyards. He also controlled eight large grain elevators and did plenty of trading at the Board. Armour sold Leiter futures until he realized that he'd been caught in a corner. He offered to make a deal and settle up for $4 million, all profit for Leiter. But Leiter refused to settle, believing he could send the price higher.

So Armour became determined to break the corner. As a seller, he was obligated to deliver wheat in Chicago at a specified time. Leiter had made sure there wasn't enough wheat available locally for Armour to buy. But there was wheat that would do the job around Minnesota, and Armour was rich enough to get it. As winter set in, he sent ice-breaking boats north to keep the water from freezing up. With the channels open, he had freighters bring grain to Chicago loaded down with 1 million bushels of wheat.

The battle between the two men played out over several months. Leiter took delivery of the wheat and kept it off the market, in elevators, to keep prices high. But high prices are like fertilizer—they make crops grow. The next summer farmers did some speculating of their own. Inspired, they grew loads of wheat, and consequently there was more than enough to meet demand. So what Armour had started, the farmers finished. When the price of wheat collapsed, Leiter's paper winnings turned to a $10-million loss. His dad bailed him out. Armour was soon distracted by another scandal involving tainted beef.

Soon after, Leiter and his speculating colleagues were immortalized in literature. In 1903 a writer named Frank Norris published the novel *The Pit*, a fictionalized take on the Leiter corner. The Leiter stand-in, Curtis Jadwin, becomes addicted to speculating in the market, which nearly destroys his life. At the climax, his destruction is played out in public as people from the city crowd into the visitors' gallery and watch him lose everything.

The next year Parker Brothers released "Pit," a game that dealt cards representing different grains. Players hit a bell and noisily attempted to corner the market. Then, in 1909, after the muck-raking classic *The Jungle* excoriated the meat packers, D. W. Griffith released *Corner in Wheat* and in fourteen silent minutes painted a picture of a callous "wheat king" who in a suit and with a cigar made a fortune on the backs of hardworking farmers and hungry children. As he celebrates over a fancy dinner, the price of bread rises and lines form. A baker turns away a mother and child unable to pay for a loaf of bread, and he turns away a group of hungry men. When they get upset, policemen run them off. The solution, to Griffith, seemed clear. His wheat king visits a grain elevator and while there receives a telegram that says he has made another $4 million and controls the world's wheat. The king pumps his fist in the air. But as he does so, he slips into the grain and is buried alive.

Hutchinson and Leiter headed up a long line of people who tried to corner their way to riches and glory. The local papers gleefully reported on the many who failed. Yet into the 1920s, the games continued. Large traders, especially one named Arthur Cutten, continued to manipulate the market. Farmers complained about erratic wheat prices. Finally the secretary of agriculture demanded that Board of Trade members oust the clique of "gamblers and scalpers" in control of the exchange. And members in the 1920s had no choice but to adopt something that they had previously resisted.

The Board of Trade members adopted a self-enforcement system called central clearing that was already in place at exchanges in Minneapolis and Kansas City and became a foundational element of futures trading. The members created an entity called the Board of Trade Clearing Corporation, which brought order to the market. This clearinghouse became an intermediary that guaranteed both sides of every trade, collecting money from losers to pay to winners. It also inspired members to watch each other. A trader put money in an account with a "clearing firm" that would be held responsible and would have to pay the clearinghouse if that trader walked away from a debt. Because the clearing firm was on the hook, it watched the trader. If he looked like a wild gambler, the clearing firm limited how much he could trade. If a trader lost money, he had to pony up more money to stay in the market. If the clearing firm couldn't pay the clearinghouse, an emergency fund or other clearing firms would be held accountable. The clearing firms became like the neighborhood watch group, always on the lookout for potential deadbeats.

This seemed to work because the exchange continued on. In 1929, when buildings exploded upward all over the Loop, built for companies selling chemicals, furniture, toothpaste, and other goods, the Board of Trade members erected their own building. At the foot of La Salle Street, they constructed a joyful Art Deco headquarters, the tallest building in the city. They would trade through the Depression and the Dust Bowl, stopping only during the Second World War, when the government capped the price of some foods. When prices were held steady, there was no need for futures or for people who traded them. For a time, the price of a membership fell to $25, and it looked like the futures exchange would die a quick death.

But the war ended, prices rebounded, members returned to La Salle Street, and the Board of Trade came back to life, as did a test case in capitalism. The exchange was simple, full of real people trading real things. Run with some democracy and a little law and order, the Chicago Board of Trade looked like a microcosm of the country—a small, intense version of the American experiment.

After the Second World War, Chicago seemed like a different place. The city of unbridled and unreasonable optimism had grown up and morphed into the city of the common, hardworking man. By the 1950s, its neighborhoods were full of brick bungalows. Residents drove their Austin Healeys down Lake Shore Drive, which ran down the side of Lake Michigan, and on weekends families took the Green Hornet streetcar to the Loop and had picnics in Grant Park, where they gawked at the Versailles-inspired Buckingham Fountain. They ambled to State Street to shop at Marshall Field's department store, and they cheered at baseball games and wrestling matches at the International Amphitheater, where women wore dresses and makeup and men wore ties and fedoras.

In 1952, A. J. Liebling from *The New Yorker* published a series of mocking articles about a year he spent living in Chicago. Poking fun at the skyline, the beaches, and the residents, he nicknamed Chicago "the Second City." But if Chicago seemed to have lost its spirit, some of it lived on inside a building on La Salle Street.

It was an unusual office building at 141 West Jackson—a tall Art Deco structure with a statue on top. The lobby was loaded with marble and nickel silver metalwork. Traders could walk in and look up at several floors, like they were looking at the decks of a cruise ship. The six-story trading room, on the fourth floor, was even more impressive. Cigar smoke and haze rose to the ceiling, and huge windows looked north down La Salle Street toward the Chicago River and the Merchandise Mart on the other side. The other walls were paneled with English oak, and an elevated chalkboard wrapped around the room attended to by men on cat-walks, covered in chalk dust. At the same level, there was a balcony for visitors to observe the goings-on. Even with the massive windows, the room seemed dim because a canyon of buildings outside blocked most sunlight.

The room was loud. It held several hundred men, many of them older, holding pipes and cigars and maybe a flask in a pocket. Some stood in front of the windows by tables with hard stone tops on which small bags of grain—samples from railcars that were sitting on tracks somewhere outside in Chicagoland—were examined. Men from companies like Pillsbury and General Mills came by, reached into the bags, and pulled out handfuls of corn, wheat, oats, and other grains. They ran the kernels through their fingers to gauge the quality, and if the price was right, they made a deal. Then the men wrote orders on forms and sent them to a railroad office in the building, arranging for the railcars to be routed to a new owner.

The deals they struck were based on the prices being determined a few steps away, in the pits, where groups of men yelled and gestured as they traded futures contracts. As they reacted to the buy and sell orders coming in, they provided a window into the bigger, hazier world of people supplying and demanding grain. After the bell rang to close the market, many adjourned to committee meetings where they discussed everything from disputes between members to the direction of the exchange to the color of the paint on the walls.

Chicago, with Lake Michigan on the east side, was a mix of people largely divided into north and south, the north being more white-collar and the south more working-class. The South Side had heavily Irish working-class neighborhoods like Bridge-port and Back of the Yards, whose residents drove hogs or cattle through the nearby stockyards and met some of the people coming through—like the Kansas cattle broker Charlie Andrews before he started trading pork belly futures. Others worked at steel mills. South Side residents cheered on the White Sox at Comiskey Park, prayed at their local parish, and warmed their bungalows at night, sometimes by burning coal. They were tight-knit and insular. And they elected politicians from their ranks to run the city.

The Board, too, had a mix of people, including executives at major grain companies that did business on the exchange. It had men who were German, Czech, Jewish, and from the North Side. But the perception became that the members who controlled the exchange and made decisions were South Side Irish. It had many independent brokers and traders, the working-class men of the financial industry who performed the tasks that made the market run. In the 1920s and 1930s, some of them had made money and moved farther south to the more suburban neighborhoods with green lawns and handsome homes. The Rock Island Line train stopped just outside the back door of the Board of Trade, and traders hopped on there and hopped off at stops like Gresham, Beverly, and Blue Island.

The list of members included McCarthys, McGuires, McKerrs, O'Briens, O'Connors, and Ryans. There was also Peter Carey, who was elected by members in the 1930s to be their president. They helped give the exchange the temperament of an Irish family— private, clannish, supportive of insiders, suspicious of outsiders. In 1938 an attorney for the grain company Cargill, when fighting with the members, complained the Board of Trade was run in "closed social club style."

The work was cyclical and less dependable than a typical job in a typical office, but members could bring in sons, nephews, and cousins, teach them the business, and pass it down. During the Second World War, when trading and opportunities to make money dried up, Peter Carey left and was elected Cook County sheriff. He died of a heart attack in 1943, his first year in that job. But his son Bernard "Bernie" Carey, who had studied to be a priest, was by then a member of the Board of Trade. Bernie flew twenty-five daylight bombing raids over Germany, came back after the war, and became a bean trader.

After the war, soldiers returned to Chicago, and some came back to the Board of Trade. It was like a second homecoming to be back in the dim room, with all the sounds, friends, and activity they had missed. They were joined by others who came to the Board for the first time after the war. Many veterans had fought, then used the GI Bill to go to school. They were just looking for work, and they found futures trading.

The board required an intense job interview. A prospective member started in an office, where he needed to have two members in good standing vouch for his character. Then the membership committee met and discussed the applicant, weeding out anyone who had a questionable financial background or seemed likely to go bankrupt. The weeding was easy when an applicant had a family member around. After that, the directors of the exchange passed around a small wooden box, slightly bigger than a cigar box. The directors dropped white marbles into the box if they approved of an applicant, and black marbles if they had concerns. The chairman of the exchange would then open a small drawer in the box and report on what he saw—usually white marbles.

When an applicant was admitted, becoming one of 1,402 members, he scrounged up a few thousand dollars to pay for a membership—to buy a "seat" in the terms of the market. Bankers didn't usually lend money for this, so traders leaned on family and friends.

Then a new trader needed another kind of sponsor—someone who would guarantee his trades. There were clearing firms for this, run in offices by people like brothers Jimmy and Charlie McKerr, a wheat trader and corn broker, respectively. They typically had a new trader put up margin money to trade, and if the new member couldn't do it, they might front him the cash. If there was a problem and a trader got in over his head, the firm was responsible. But if the trader caught on, every time he bought or sold a futures contract he paid the clearing firm a fee. As a new member traded more and more contracts, he naturally paid more fees.

There was no guarantee of what a new trader would do on the trading floor. Theoretically he could go into a pit, lose money, disappear, and stick the McKerrs with a debt to pay to the clearinghouse. But the exchange was small. Most men who joined were brought in by a friend or relative. The McKerrs weren't too worried about a customer disappearing on them. They often told a new trader to trade small to start. Then they sent him to the trading floor.

A new trader made a typical progression on the floor. If he had someone watching out for him, he stood next to that person and learned the business. If he was less connected, he started in a small pit for rye, lard, or oats. It was easy to break into the oat pit, which was small, with just a dozen or so laid-back men standing around. If they were in a good mood, the older men might go easy on a new guy. The oat market fluctuated slowly and only slightly. That gave him time to learn the correct shouts, nods of the head, and hand signals that it took to make a trade. He could work up the nerve to make a trade and risk some money.

After a time, a new trader often graduated to a bigger pit, mainly corn or wheat, with dozens of people, including some wide, solid-looking men. These two pits differed mainly by how the market moved. The corn price lumbered along like the old Ford car of the trading floor. It didn't move much unless there was an interesting weather or crop report or some other news that would cause it to move. The wheat pit was the Cadillac of the floor and moved a bit faster, although as Americans ate more meat and less wheat, the wheat pit slowed down.

In the corn and wheat pits, it was important to learn to avoid the psychological traps that caught traders, like being too proud to admit a mistake. When a man lost money, it was best to take the loss and move on. That was surprisingly hard to do. Also, a new trader had to learn not to talk about how much money he made or lost. To listen to what people said, nobody ever made a dime. Their mothers taught them to not brag, but there was also a legitimate business reason to keep quiet. A trader needed a poker face in a futures pit. When the bell rang, a trader had no friends. If a man was under stress and in financial trouble and showed fear in his eyes, he was like a wounded antelope waiting for the lions. Traders looked for shoulder twitches, lip-licking, restless legs, and other nervous habits that might show who among them had become prey.

In those postwar years, traders often wound their way to the soybean pit, known as the "bean" pit. It had started in 1936 and was still the new pit on the floor. If the corn pit was the Ford of the trading floor and the wheat pit the Cadillac, then the bean pit was on its way to becoming a Maserati. It would become the pit for people who liked action and adventure and risk.

An active pit magnetically drew traders from around the floor, especially when one of the legendary traders put in an appearance. Daniel Rice, for instance, worked mostly from an office but was so well known and respected that he could influence trading just by standing in a pit and letting others guess his intentions. He was famous for, among other things, having cornered the rye market in 1944. Some said he sank a boat of rye to do it.

There was Joe Dimon, a tall man with a southern accent who also hung out in the bean pit. A wild trader, he was usually in the process of making or losing a lot of money. The government had a limit on how many futures any one person could buy or sell, but Dimon had ways of exceeding that limit. He often had a briefcase full of cash nearby so that he'd be ready for an impromptu craps game or a bet—on anything, including raindrops. Dimon was nice when he was broke and could be mean when he was rich. He didn't recognize his own flaws, and that was the fastest way at the Board to end up broke.

Every man in the pit had a different job or trading strategy. The floor brokers traded for customers, which were usually companies rather than individuals. Someone from the company would telephone a brokerage desk on the floor of the Board of Trade.

Then a man at that desk would write down the order on a five-by-eight-inch order sheet, with a color specific to the firm. He would hand it to a runner to take to the pit and hand to a floor broker. When the time was right, the broker, like an auctioneer opening an auction, would yell out the order. If he was selling contracts, he'd put his palm out with the number of fingers indicating the number he was selling. If he was buying, his palm would face in. Someone else would yell and gesture in return, agreeing on the price the customer wanted. Then the floor broker would write the details—the clearinghouse, the broker's trading acronym, the number of contracts, the price—on the same order sheet and toss it onto the floor. A runner would pick it up and take it back to the desk, where a clerk who was a member of the exchange would call the customer to let the firm know that its order was filled. The order sheet went to a clerk who put the information on punch cards. At the end of the day, the clerk would take those cards to the clearing firm and ultimately the clearinghouse, which matched up the trades like socks, making sure every buyer and seller was part of a pair.

Floor brokers could also trade for themselves, with their own money. Many people on the floor did only that, using different strategies. Some were scalpers. They were like fast chess players playing timed games on the street. Scalpers tried to anticipate where the market was going in the short term by watching other traders and listening to the sounds on the floor. They bought and sold constantly, trying to make a few dollars on each trade and to make as many trades as possible so as to go home even at the end of the day.

Others were position traders who placed intermediate-term trades, holding them for a week to a few weeks. Still others were long-term traders who might make a trade and hold it for several months. They took bigger risks for potentially bigger profits. For them, unlike the scalpers, it helped to know something about what they were trading, like the weather and the fundamental conditions.

For example, in the bean pit, soybeans, a relatively new crop in the United States, got attention thanks to a man a few hours south named Augustus Staley. He saw that soybeans were cheaper than corn but offered more protein. So he processed, or crushed, them into two main products: soybean oil, which housewives used for cooking, and soybean meal, which farmers used to quickly plump up chickens and hogs, which housewives cooked too. While the government had programs that created surpluses in corn and wheat, the soybean market was subject to the whim of supply and demand. For a position trader in the bean pit, it helped to know how many acres of beans were being grown or stored and the condition of the crop. It also helped to know of potential buyers. Some traders said a man named Colonel Harland Sanders was out setting up restaurants and might boost the demand for soybean meal, as he needed more chickens to fry in his pressure cookers.

And there were the spreaders, who often had the nicest homes and cars. An axiom repeated on the floor was that if you were going to last in the business you had to learn to spread. The spreaders could turn the business of risk-taking into a job that was at times almost mechanical and routine. They bought one contract that seemed undervalued and sold a related one. For example, many spreaders bought bean futures delivering in July, figuring prices would rise that month as crops were used up. Simultaneously, they sold bean futures delivering in November, figuring prices would go down at harvest time. Each side of the trade was called a "leg." Spreading was usually a reliable way to make money. When it didn't work for some reason—if prices fell instead of rising in July—the spreader had some time to get out of the position, to "leg out" of that side, with his hide intact. Having wagered on the market going both up and down, he had some protection. "Better spread than dead," they'd say.

In Chicago it was rare for someone to simply walk in off the street and join the exchange. Hardly anyone in recent years had ever heard about it happening. Rather young men usually found the business through family. Eddie O'Connor, a tall, black-haired son of a cop who walked the beat on the West Side of Chicago, had flown in the back of a bomber during the war. After returning home, he worked as an usher, collected train tickets on the "L," went to law school, and worked in insurance. His cousin, whose foot had been blown off in the war, was a broker and showed him around there. O'Connor fit in well enough. He was Irish, although he was from the West Side, not the South Side like some running the place. The West Side had lighter industry, like candy factories. He could smell the stockyards only when the wind blew just so. A few years later, O'Connor would sponsor his brother Billy, just back from Korea.

Those who didn't have family at the Board could still work their way in. George Cashman, also from the West Side, got in because he had been a runner at the Board of Trade in the 1930s. He found members to sponsor him, then Cashman brought in two younger brothers—Gene, a park policeman, joined the rye pit. Eddie, who filled soybean oil orders by day, remained a police detective at night.

Lee Stern, who went to Roosevelt University a few blocks east, saw an ad posted outside the student lounge for a part-time job at the Board of Trade, which he'd heard about from a neighbor of his aunt. Knowing he could work in the morning before his classes started at 2:00 PM, Stern took a job as a runner at the Board for $25 a week, ferrying orders to brokers for Merrill Lynch. A few months later, he became a phone clerk making $40 a week. After buying a membership, using money from his mother's war bonds, he became a spreader in the bean pit.

Henry Shatkin, who had known Lee Stern in high school, heard that Stern was there and figured he could be as successful. Shatkin was a gambler who, among other games, liked dice and poker. He got to the Board and before long lost all his money. Then he found an ongoing poker game played every night at an apartment in the Rush Street nightlife district; in five months he made $20,000—reduced to $12,000 after bad checks bounced. It was enough to come back to the Board, where an older trader took Shatkin aside and taught him to be a spreader.

A few others would follow them, including Les Rosenthal, who was the son of a man who made floral-printed slipcovers for the chairs and couches of North Side housewives. He, too, would start as a clerk, working before his classes at Roosevelt University.

However, when men found their way to the building at the foot of La Salle Street, they were sucked into it. In the years after the war, young men went there and found themselves learning things not usually taught in downtown office buildings. They learned that farmers liked to drink liquor and that flax seeds were oily and sticky and fun to throw down the back of someone's shirt as a prank.

And the traders learned a lot about each other, far more than most workers in polite society learned about their colleagues. As the traders stood on the trading floor for any length of time, their days, money, and relationships were quickly intertwined. In the pits and the clearing offices, they learned who remained calm under pressure and who cracked under it. They learned who had money in the bank and who was barely scraping by. They learned who was honest and who would later argue, falsely, that he had never made a losing trade. They also learned this information was useful and a currency of its own.

When they learned who to trust, they stuck by those people. They swapped stories in upstairs offices, the smoking room, and nearby bars. They served on committees together, and they became like cousins in an extended family, often staying closest to the people who had helped bring them into the business.

The newer members were all a bit like Jack from the children's story about the beanstalk, having discovered that beans could be magical and lead places. But most had modest hopes for the future. They saw that beans, when traded on paper, could pay bills and support families. That's why in the 1950s, the few men who had found their way into the Board of Trade, if they did well enough, stayed there. They settled in as members of the insular, commodity-centered clan.

Eggs   +0.03

At the clubby Board of Trade, a few members stuck out. Some might have expected them to work at another exchange in town, one that few Board of Trade members paid any attention to. It was a few blocks away, at the corner of Washington and Franklin, housed in a handsome if grimy early skyscraper with CHICAGO MERCANTILE EXCHANGE written in the stone facade. The Mercantile Exchange, usually just called "the Merc," had five hundred members, many of whom were Jewish.

To be clear, both exchanges had people of various religions and cultures. But the Board became associated with its Irish members, and the Merc with its Jewish members. The joke was that if Murray was your last name, you belonged at the Board, and if Murray was your first name, you belonged at the Merc. Some members complained that it was easy to overstate the impact of religion, and the members were certainly also separated by the different products they traded. The Board had men with cigars who bought and sold grain. The Merc had men with cigars who bought and sold butter and eggs, which were more perishable products and gave the trade a sense of urgency.

The Merc started in 1874 as the Chicago Produce Exchange, an institution built in the wreckage of the Great Fire. When its members fought in 1898, a group split off and formed another exchange, the Chicago Butter and Egg Board. Conflict also arose among the members of the new board, but they stayed together and converted into the Chicago Mercantile Exchange in 1919.

In 1928 the Mercantile Exchange moved into a new building of its own on Franklin Street, but the map meant nothing. For practical purposes, Franklin was an extension of Fulton Street, a strip of road nearby, a few blocks north, and west over the Chicago River. It got particularly interesting a few blocks in when Fulton Street crossed Halsted Street. For nearly a mile, food wholesale companies lined both sides of the street, most of them in low brick buildings.

This neighborhood represented a large proportion of the nation's food hub. Food products came into Chicago, then went out to the rest of the country. The eggs, butter, and poultry came through Fulton Street, a busy place where parking was impossible to find. The vehicle of anyone lucky enough to find a spot was likely to be scraped by a passing truck. By 5:00 AM on a typical day, the street was as crowded as Marshall Field's department store in the days leading up to Christmas. Men in bloodstained aprons stood on loading docks, looking as though they'd climbed out of vats of red paint. City inspectors stepped through the puddles left by melting ice. As workers packed boxes of chicken onto trucks, Mafia men picked up feathers from the poultry companies to sell to a nearby mattress factory.

In all of the buildings, men cut deals. They arranged homes for thousands of pounds of food, they argued over a few cents per pound, and they operated with cash. The whole neighborhood reeked. The smell could put a weak man in a coma—until he learned to appreciate that the odor was the smell of money. After that, the stench bothered him for five minutes on Monday morning and then he ignored it for the rest of the week.

The first four blocks housed meat and fish firms. Poultry company workers took crates of live chickens off trucks. When chickens escaped down the street, the workers used hangers to try to grab them by the neck and bring them back. They took the chickens in an elevator to a room on the top floor, where they slit the birds' throats and threw the carcasses into a chute. They rarely missed because they practiced the shot all day long. The chute dumped the chicken carcasses into a cement tub full of ice in the basement. Then they were sent to a different, cleaner building to be sliced and packaged.

At the corner of Morgan Street was Fulton Market Cold Storage, a ten-story brick warehouse that was like an anchor of the neighborhood. Railroad tracks passed just one block north of Fulton, and one track led directly into the warehouse's receiving area, where men pulled boxes of beef, frozen slabs of pork, and other foodstuffs off railcars and pushed it all on dollies into a large elevator. They had to wear heavy coats while they stacked the food up in giant rooms, which ranged in temperature from chilly to deeply frozen. Almost everyone on the street brought product there and stored it when their coolers were full.

The four blocks of Fulton Street beyond Fulton Market Cold Storage, from Morgan to Racine Streets, were lined with companies that were all, somehow or other, in the egg business. There was Peter Fox and Sons, where Peter's nine sons sold turkey, butter, and eggs. There was G. H. Miller, which sold fresh eggs by the carload, run by Gil Miller, a tall, beefy guy with a full head of hair. There was a company originally run by three Becker brothers, Mike, Dave, and Max. They also sold butter. On hot days, like a kid licking ice cream, short and stout Dave Becker licked a stick of butter to cool off.

The street was incestuous. Michael Becker married the sister of small and dapper Saul Stone, also an egg man on the street. One of their daughters married Gil Miller. Farther along was Charles K. Schulte, an egg company owned by a man of the same name. Across the street from Schulte was Sol Rich, who plowed money he made on eggs into real estate, including a cold storage warehouse on the Chicago River. To save money, he lifted manual forklifts of eggs himself.

Many of these establishments were in the business of buying and selling eggs, an industry where an immigrant with a few dollars and a few contacts could make a business. Every week farmers with chickens packed up cases of eggs, put them on a truck, and shipped them to Fulton Street. An egg dealer or two on Fulton may have slipped a few dollars to a trailer truck driver who, in return, might have told his boss that he hit a few bumps on the highway. That way, the seller would shave a few dollars from the bill. Either way, from there the egg dealers sold fresh eggs to grocers like National Tea Company, Jewel, and many independent grocers. They shipped eggs to East Coast cities.

They stored some eggs in a cooler or cold storage room in anticipation of better prices. The neighborhood was dotted with the cold storage warehouses where dealers put a light coating of vegetable oil on the eggs' shells and put them in a warehouse at thirty-eight to forty degrees, where they could last for months. When prices were higher, the dealers delivered eggs to hotels, restaurants, hospitals, and other customers around town, trying to resell them for a few cents more than they had paid. Taxes were low because egg selling was a cash business. Although, when a dealer named Ira Zeidman delivered eggs to a Chinese restaurant whose owner didn't have cash, he was paid with Chinese food instead.

Some of the eggs were broken for other uses. Truck drivers from various Fulton Street merchants picked up whole eggs from egg dealers and delivered them to egg-breaking companies, such as one run by the Schneider brothers, Sam and Sol. Sam looked like a short, pugnacious sailor with a Yiddish accent. Sol was frailer and had thick glasses.

In their egg-breaking plant, employees in a dark room flash-candled the eggs, giving them a quick look to find defects. They placed the eggs on a conveyer belt, and women on either side stood at stainless steel tables with egg-breaking equipment. As the belt moved, each woman picked eggs off the belt, broke them open, and filled cups with the yolks and whites. Then she smelled the eggs to make sure they were good. If so, she dumped the cup into a stainless steel bucket. When the bucket was filled, another employee walked it to the "floor lady," who also smelled the eggs. If they smelled okay, she dumped them into a hopper, a large receptacle with a series of screens to catch impurities. The eggs were pumped into stainless steel vats where an agitator kept them circulating. Then a worker poured thirty pounds of egg liquid into a tin, sealed the tin with a rubber mallet, and sent it to the cooler or the freezer. These "frozen" eggs, as they were called, went to bakeries and pie, noodle, and mayonnaise makers.

Although whole eggs could be left in cold storage for a few months before going bad or shrinking inside the shell, and frozen eggs could be left for years, egg prices could change while the eggs sat in storage, and that was a headache for egg men. Prices fluctuated because eggs were seasonal. There were a lot of fresh eggs in the spring, the equivalent of harvest time. And there was an egg shortage in the winter, when hens laid less. But it was also difficult to predict how many eggs housewives would buy at the store in any given week.

While his eggs were in storage, the dealer could hedge with futures to help him budget. If he was lucky, the price of eggs rose while they were in storage. If he was unlucky, the price of eggs fell. So egg men on the street used egg futures like short-term insurance. A dealer sold a futures contract as a hedge if he thought prices might fall. That way, if the price of eggs dropped, he bought back the futures contract for a profit that canceled out what he had lost on the eggs.

Every time a man who was not a member of the Merc called his broker to do this, it cost $35 or so. Whereas if he joined, he could trade with discounted rates. That was how many egg dealers found their way to the Merc.

The building was still lovely in the 1950s, but plainer than the opulent Board of Trade. The lobby had a small cigar and candy store run by a man who doubled as a bookie. He stood near a marble staircase that led to the trading floor, a three-story room that looked vaguely like a high school gym, but one filled by a cloud of smoke. In the summer, with no air conditioning, the trading floor got hot. It had chalkboards on the marble walls, parquet floors festooned with cigarette and cigar burns, and brass cuspidors for tobacco. Its arched, two-story windows overlooked Franklin Street. Half the room had rows of desks with phones whose lights flashed when someone was on the line. On a small third-floor balcony, men from around the city came to sit and dream about how they'd trade if only they had the money, and a few gamblers came to use the prices from the floor as inspiration for their bets at the numbers racket (the lottery).

The Merc was like a miniature version of Fulton Street, with many of the same people. To join the club, an applicant bought a membership and went in front of the membership committee, but that was a perfunctory exercise because most people already knew each other. The club included some Becker brothers and sons, including the sons Sam and Phil, who married sisters and bought homes next to each other in Glencoe, a northern suburb. Saul Stone and Sol Rich were there, as were several of the Fox sons. One, Bert Fox, sat at a desk and whacked passersby with his canes. His nephew Harold Fox walked around with a burnt tie and a cigarette in his mouth as ashes fell on his collar and protruding stomach. Sam Schneider was there, regularly paying fines to the exchange for his loud swearing. And Sol Schneider's son Maurie was there, wearing a badge that read "MORIE," a misspelled version of his name because trading acronyms could be only five letters long.

The man walking around with a white carnation in his lapel was Miles Friedman, who brokered deals in the cash egg business from his office. Butter dealer John McCarthy was from Ireland, and he had two young men working with him—his son and son-in-law. Sydney Maduff, an egg man originally from Iowa, also worked there with his sons. There was friendly Hyman "Hi" Henner, who came from the Ukraine in 1906. He had two sons with him as well, Bill and David. Henner was a broker on the floor, as were some of the other members, buying and selling for customers.

Every morning the members dropped off their overcoats in a coatroom in the corridor. Then, wearing suits and small name tags, they went to the trading floor and haggled in front of the chalkboards, eventually ending up in several pits. When the market opened, they stood on the floor in an octagonal pit in front of chalkboards and shouted to a man standing on a raised catwalk. He had his back to the traders but could recognize their voices. If the market for eggs was fifty cents a dozen, a member might yell out a bid, "Buy two at even," meaning he would buy two contracts at 50 cents. The board man would write the bid on the "buy" chalkboard. Someone else might yell out an offer, which the board man would write on the "sell" board. When a bid and an offer matched, he wrote up the trade on a board in the middle, detailing the price, the quantity, and the trading acronyms of the buyer and seller.

Usually one or two of the traders thought prices would go up, while the others thought prices would go down. Sometimes they took a break and went to the washroom, where they got their shoes shined while they contemplated egg prices.

The clearing firms were owned by most of the major egg dealers. They backed traders and in theory maintained margin money from customers. In practice, however, the clearing firms were casual about collecting money because customers were mostly friends and relatives. If a man they knew made a bad trade and ran out of money, he'd usually get another chance the next day. Each afternoon they wrote the total gains and losses of their customers on Mercantile forms and took those sheets to a few people working in the clearinghouse in a large room one floor above the trading floor. Sheets were due each day by 3:00 PM.

A man who was not a member, named Everette B. Harris, watched the scene. The traders called him by the nickname E.B., either fondly or sometimes with a snarl. In the small club, Harris stood apart. He had grown up on a farm in southern Illinois and worked for four years as secretary at the Board of Trade before being lured to the Merc in 1953. He was tall, with glasses and a well-tailored air. A reporter later described him as having the "square profile of an aging matinee idol." He was a man in the middle, neither Catholic nor Jewish but Presbyterian. He talked corn with farmers, haggled with egg dealers, and sipped martinis with government officials in Washington. He walked around the trading floor and sat in his adjoining office with a sense of fearlessness.

Men from the Commodity Exchange Authority, a division of the Department of Agriculture, ostensibly oversaw the futures business, but they had no idea what was going on there. Sometimes they came to the Merc in three-piece suits, stood next to Harris, and looked confused. Everyone knew regulators relied on Harris to tell them if anything needed fixing. So Harris had a lot of power at the Merc, a power he kept close.

The egg and butter men lived in their own small world, with Fulton Street on one side and the Merc on the other. On the trading floor, they watched the clerks feed orders to the traders in the pit, and they learned to read poker faces to figure out who was buying or selling.

The Merc was the embarrassing little sister to the Board, different from it in many ways. The Board was full of people from Chicago's South Side, whereas the Merc was run by people from the North Side. They banked at separate Chicago banks, the Board with Continental, the Merc with Harris Bank. The Board was called Irish, the Merc was called Jewish. The Merc was unquestionably the wilder, less reputable of the two exchanges. And that's what led it to change.

Onions   +0.04

Trading egg futures was a game. The object for the people playing was to guess the price by anticipating supply and demand and figuring out how many eggs would be left in storage in the fall and winter. The game had rules. The only eggs that mattered were those delivered to storage facilities that had been approved by the Mercantile Exchange, and they had to be delivered there by a certain date. If eggs arrived too old or had been kept in a non-approved facility, they were eliminated.

The egg game also had a season. Technically the market was open year-round, but there were slow months when it was tough to learn much about the egg supply. You needed information to play. In September, when the first eggs were taken out of storage and delivered to buyers, trading heated up. Then the game was on for four wild months. If a trader lost money one month, he had until January to try again and reverse his losses. As the days and weeks ticked toward a decisive conclusion in January, however, and the price of eggs bounced around as traders put the final pieces of the puzzle together, they got more anxious. During the last days, trading in the pit got feverish.

At the end of January the contract expired, sellers delivered eggs to buyers, and storage stocks were depleted. If a trader had bet wrong and lost money, it was too late to do anything. January was the end of the line. He had to wait until September drew closer for the fun to begin again.

During the slow months, members at the Merc needed other things to trade to keep themselves busy. Some traded butter, but that was a small affair. In the 1930s the government had introduced the first of several programs that regulated the price of butter. Those programs made butter prices stable and predictable, and that meant that dealers didn't need to use futures contracts to lock in prices.

At a fixed time each day, butter and egg dealers engaged in a ritual to trade their products at what was called a "cash" board on the trading floor. Cash product represented actual product like butter and eggs, as opposed to the paper trade made in futures. In the trading room, a Merc employee stood in front of one of the chalkboards surrounding the trading floor. Butter dealers told him the prices at which they would buy or sell butter, and he wrote them up in chalk. A few minutes later, he'd call out, "Any more trading in butter or eggs?" three times and look at the butter and egg dealers sitting at their desks to get their response. After a wave and a nod, trading was over. And butter trading was on its way out.

Some traded futures on potatoes, but more traded futures on onions. Both of those products came from a nearby area of the city called South Water Market. The grain traders originally met on South Water Street, just off the Chicago River, but the food business had split up by the early 1900s. The butter and egg men went to Fulton Street, and local farmers sold goods like flowers, sweet corn, and beets on nearby Randolph Street. South Water Street was left to the sellers, many of them Greeks and Italians, in the produce business, like a Sicilian named Dominick Testa. He started with three dollars and a basket, then bought a horse-drawn wagon and then a truck. When his business grew, he brought in his young sons to work with him.

The South Water Street men bought produce from faraway places like California and Idaho. In 1926, when the city built a double-decker street called Wacker Drive—which wrapped around the burgeoning Loop and shunted traffic and trucks to a lower level—the merchants left South Water Street and opened a new market two miles south at Fifteenth Street. Location aside, however, they continued to call it the South Water Market.

The market had a twelve-story building with brokers' offices and a barber shop, and it included six long buildings with two hundred stores, each of which was little more than a loading dock and a refrigerator. They were mostly produce stores, with a few hot dog manufacturers, fish sellers, and a canned goods merchant thrown into the mix.

Every morning, six days a week, produce arrived on railcars at a gigantic rail yard nearby, where more than two thousand cars of fruits and vegetables sat on the tracks. A few dozen buyers gathered around and bid for the food coming off the cars. They bought crates of four dozen heads of lettuce packed in ice, or 18 cantaloupes, or 150 oranges, or 75 lemons. They hauled what they bought across the street to the stores, where wholesalers, restaurants, and grocers came through to shop when the market opened at 3:00 AM. Customers came with trucks, workers cursed, and vendors haggled as every man tried to outbid or outsell the person next to him. When the morning rush was over, all the buyers and sellers refueled at one of the seven or so restaurants across the street, where a man could get a hearty and super-fresh lunch for $1.50. By afternoon the day was over.

Some of the merchants were in the potato and onion business. They unloaded burlap sacks of potatoes and onions from the railcars and reloaded some onto trains or trucks bound for New Orleans and other cities. They took other sacks to their stores, where they repacked the potatoes and onions into smaller bags, packing up whatever customers wanted, such as special boxes of two-inch-long potatoes if that was what a hotel or restaurant had asked for.

Most produce had to be sold and eaten right away, but potatoes and onions—and apples for that matter—could last for some time in the refrigerator. So, if they believed that the onion price was too low, merchants moved some sacks into cold storage warehouses, speculating that the price would go up. If they were right, prices would rise and they made an extra dollar per sack. The warehouse men liked the business because they had room to fill. Most eggs were out of cold storage by January, although the smell of onions, unfortunately, lingered in coolers long after the season ended in March.

When the Merc introduced markets in potatoes and onions in 1942, some of the South Water men, like the egg and butter men, who also had perishable product on ice, made their way to the trading floor on Franklin Street. One man who came was Jack Carl, known as Chicago's "apple man" because he sold more of those than anyone. Carl sold mostly fruit, but he would trade anything that made him some money. Another new trader was Sam Siegel, a medium-sized man with a fairly large potato and onion business.

The exchange was quiet during the Second World War. Most egg men were busy making money without futures, selling eggs to feed the hungry soldiers in Europe and the Pacific. Slowly, however, the onion market took hold.

Onions were fated to trade in Chicago. The name of the city was derived from *shikaakwa*, the Native American word for a stinky, wild leek plant that grew around the river, although the Merc's members preferred to trade the hard and pungent variety that farmers grew on small plots from Minnesota to New York. In Hollandale, Minnesota, growers planted onion seeds in late April and harvested onions in September. They sold some right away, but the world only needed so many onions at one time. So growers stored the rest in warehouses or sheds on their farms. Then, sometime between January and March, they would load up their trucks with boxes of onions and haul them to the local cooperative. A crew there examined them, looking for bruises or dirt stains, and divided the onions by size. They loaded them into fifty-pound sacks, put them on railcars, and shipped them out to South Water Market.

The egg traders didn't know much about onions, but they knew about seasonal price shifts, and they knew how to trade futures.

So they traded onion and potato futures too. They liked trading onion futures because egg trading pretty much ended in January but onion trading continued in earnest until March, filling the gap for a couple of additional months.

Even before the Merc officially formed, butter and egg dealers played trading games. In 1915 the board of directors at what was then the Chicago Butter and Egg Board banned futures for sixty days in an experiment that some members said might curb corners. In 1917 they banned futures again after twenty-five men were indicted for trying to monopolize the market. The board suspended futures trading yet again in August 1921, and that December, after an alleged corner carried out by a clique of brokers, a judge suspended futures trading temporarily.

At the Board of Trade, it had become more difficult over the years for individual traders, or even a group of them, to corner a market. There was simply too much grain. It was still possible, though difficult, to squeeze the market by holding product off the market and buying futures to drive the price up. The traders who were most likely to pull it off were large grain firms—"commercials," in trader lingo—like Dreyfus, Continental Grain, and Cargill. They had the best idea of supply, the money to buy a lot of grain, and the connections to disguise their purchases. In the grain market, a deep-pocketed trader who could afford to buy grain and store it for years had a huge advantage.

But the Merc had smaller markets and perishable products. It was cheaper to try to corner a market because a trader didn't have to buy as much. It was also easier to keep the trading of smaller amounts a secret, which was crucial to pulling off a corner. Because the products were perishable and couldn't be stored, the trader didn't have to worry about people sitting on inventory and suddenly dumping it on the market. And at the Merc it also didn't take as long to find out if a corner attempt had worked.

Whenever someone cornered the market, the game unfolded over the course of several weeks or months. In the first weeks, a trader or group of traders quietly bought futures. Sometimes they disguised their orders by funneling them through different brokers in the pit. As their position grew, others in the pit caught on. It would come to a head in January for eggs, and in March for onions. When egg dealer Ira Zeidman joined the Merc, he learned quickly that if he didn't want to get caught in a corner, he needed to close out his position before that last month. The last minutes of trading in a contract were the moments of reckoning. For a trader or customer who was trapped and trying to extricate himself, the last thirty seconds could feel like a week.

Many men on the trading floor lost money in market corners and squeezes, but they tolerated the games because everyone on the floor knew the rules and played along. They also enjoyed telling stories of sly moves and double-crosses, and the stories got better and more colorful with every telling.

There was the old one about Miles Friedman, head of a butter, produce, and egg company named after himself. Friedman was elected president of the exchange in 1939 and used the position to his advantage. The story is that he sauntered by the chalkboards where the bids and offers for egg futures were written and casually bought all the futures available. After he bought them all, he pulled out a telegram with the news that the U.S. Department of Agriculture was starting a school lunch program—news that was sure to send the market higher. The telegram was addressed to the head of the Chicago Mercantile Exchange. Rather than circulate the news, he had used it to make money for himself, at the expense of everyone who sold him futures. Friedman's trading acronym, which he wrote on trading cards, was "MF," and some clerks used to say, for instance, "Siegel sold five at fifty to Mother Fucker." No doubt some felt that name was fitting.

But the best was the story about Roy Simmons, a large trader from Oswego, New York. On the floor he traded for himself, but he worked through many clearing firms, so that no one ever knew exactly how many futures contracts he had bought or sold. He sent some orders through floor brokers whom he instructed to look for his signals: to buy futures, for instance, when he lifted a pen, or to sell when he put a cigar in his mouth.

Simmons was part of a clique that tried to corner onions by buying what looked like a controlling supply of the market. On the last day of trading, the clique didn't show up, and everyone in the pit knew why. They had locked themselves together in a room at the Sherman Hotel, a lovely but fading stone-and-brick hotel close to the trading floor. There they could watch each other at a crucial time, to make sure no one broke the corner.

A corner or squeeze was a fragile thing. If it worked and made money, the people involved wanted to make sure their profits were evenly divided. If it didn't work and lost money, they wanted to sell futures in an orderly way and split losses fairly. The members knew each other, and they knew better than to trust each other. At the Merc, "Trust me, trust me" was just code for "Screw you."

In one version of the onion story, Simmons decided to sell his futures without anyone else knowing. He went to the window and lowered the blinds, which was a signal to an accomplice who was waiting outside. The accomplice then ran to the trading floor and sold Simmons's futures, making him money and screwing his co-conspirators. In another version, he tapped on the pipes to communicate with an accomplice. And in yet another version of the story, Simmons and the others were in a room with a single phone, which they used to call their brokers and ask what was happening in the pit. By design, they had no privacy. Simmons got on the phone with his broker on the floor and asked for the latest. Then he coughed. That cough was the signal to sell his futures. Whichever version of events was true, Simmons double-crossed his co-conspirators.

They didn't hold it against him forever, as they might have done down the block. At the Board of Trade, some said traders got "Irish Alzheimer's": They forgot everything but a grudge. Merc members also held grudges, if not for as long, because making and losing money was personal. Futures trading was a zero-sum game. When one person made money, it meant that another person lost money.

And when a man on the floor lost money, he knew who on the floor had essentially taken it from him.

Business was personal to onion growers too. The games that traders played in the pit had repercussions in farmland. In 1950 the price of onions fell from $5.05 to 44 cents in seven months, a decline that was difficult to ascribe entirely to supply and demand. Futures and supply were intertwined. When prices in the pit got high, onion farmers planted more onions to take advantage of that, and overplanting led to gluts. When prices were low, farmers were unhappy and felt that onions were underpriced.

Growers complained with anonymous phone calls and telegrams, or so said the Merc's public relations man, S. L. Austin, when defending the traders in a newspaper editorial in April 1953. He insisted that manipulating the market "would have been very difficult indeed." But a lawyer for the Chicago Potato Jobbers Association, whose members also sold onions, followed up with the rebuttal that onion futures trading had crippled the industry. And when William Piowaty, a grumpy, older produce dealer who belonged to the Merc, told *The Packer*, an industry publication, that traders had manipulated the contract, the Merc fined him $200 and revoked his trading privileges for a year. He, in turn, complained that June to the *Chicago Daily Tribune* that the penalty was retribution and "very un-American."

Piowaty took up a collection to fund a campaign against onion futures. He and other men in the onion business got the attention of congressmen, and in July 1955 Congress added onions to the list of commodities that the Commodity Exchange Authority could regulate. That overlooked division of the Department of Agriculture had jurisdiction over farm-product futures, and it had the right to crack down when given a reason. Later that year Piowaty got what he needed—a clear example of what was going on at 110 North Franklin Street to show the Commodity Exchange Authority.

The manipulation involved several on the floor, but two got nabbed. One was Sam Siegel, the son of an Orthodox rabbi and the owner of cold storage facilities in a suburb next to Chicago's then-new O'Hare Airport. The other was Vincent Kosuga, a five-foot-four onion grower from New York.

Kosuga had bought a farm that no one else wanted in Pine Island, in the shadows of the Catskills, and turned it into five thousand acres of onions, celery, and lettuce. He had an enormous shed on his property, and inside it he kept huge piles of onions with two large fans blowing on them to keep them dry. He sold produce to Campbell's Soup and the U.S. Army, among others. When he started trading wheat at the Board of Trade, he lost all his money and had to borrow money from a friend to cover his losses. Kosuga promised his wife that he would stop trading, but then he got hooked again trading onions at the Merc. For several years, he flew to Chicago on Monday to trade and then back to New York on Thursday to farm.

Kosuga was one of the liveliest characters the Merc had ever seen. On his land, he had expanded a café into a restaurant called the Jolly Onion Inn, where he was the chef. His mother was a Russian Jew who had been taken in by nuns and converted. Kosuga, a dedicated Catholic, gave so much to the Vatican that he had private audiences with three popes and said he rode in the pope's private elevator. But whatever god he worshiped, he was a man with no fear. He carried a .38 revolver and a billy club. He drove stock cars, and was frightening behind the wheel. Once, he gave Roy Simmons a ride to Oswego, New York, in his plane and, after dropping him off, continued on until the plane ran out of gas and crashed. Kosuga ended up in a full body cast, but insisted on getting out of his hospital bed and going home.

After a particularly good year, Kosuga bought new Buicks for the handful of brokers he used at the Merc. One year he presented a broker named Nate Wertheimer—who was at one point a chairman of the Merc—with a big, fancy Cadillac. Fifteen minutes later, they were driving down Michigan Avenue when Kosuga, in the backseat, put his dirty feet on the ceiling of the car. Wertheimer told him to take his feet off the ceiling of his car. "Your car?" Kosuga asked, and stuck his feet through the canvas ceiling.

On the trading floor he was crafty. One time he bought onion futures and needed the price to go up. So he bribed the local U.S. weather bureau to issue a frost warning for the region. That sent the price higher. The temperature in those regions never got below fifty degrees.

Stories about corners were like sexual exploits—they grew more tawdry with every telling. But one was genuinely seedy enough to make the legal record. In the fall of 1955, Kosuga and Siegel bought enough onions and onion futures to control 98 percent of the onions in Chicago. When the market was high, they called a handful of people in the onion business, including a company owned by John Richard "Jack" Simplot, a big potato grower in Idaho. Kosuga and Siegel made a deal with these growers: They would buy some of the onions, and in return Kosuga and Siegel would keep buying as well and keep the price high, perhaps as high as $4 a bag. If the growers refused, the duo would dump the onions on the market and decimate prices, which would hurt the growers. The growers purchased some onions.

But Kosuga and Siegel double-crossed the onion growers. Onion farmers grew more onions to sell at high prices. The duo joined the sellers, knowing the price would go down, and prepared to deliver onions that they had said they would hold off the market. In March 1956, at the end of the onion season, they helped drive prices down to ten cents a contract and made millions on the trades.

The price got so low that onions were worth less than the bags that held them. Many farmers went bankrupt. In Hollandale, Minnesota, growers angrily plowed the onions back into the fields they came from. In Chicago, cars on tracks at the rail yard were full of worthless onions, and their unlucky owners had to pay rent to keep them there until they figured out what to do with them. Maurie Schneider tried giving onions to orphanages, but that lightened his load by only a few bags. He gave some onions to a friend who owned gas stations to give away as a promotion for buying gas. On Fulton Street, dealers gave away onions free with egg purchases. The butter dealer John McCarthy fed onions to hogs and sold the bags. Many ended up paying to have their onions hauled away and trashed.

Regulators investigated and filed a complaint against Kosuga and Siegel. Kosuga hired an expensive lawyer and insisted, "If it's against the law to make money in the United States, then I'm guilty." But onion growers were fed up. They wanted the futures market killed. "Supply and demand no longer make the market. Now it is done by the gamblers," wrote John Zerfas of Eaton Rapids, Michigan, to the *Chicago Daily Tribune* in March 1957, saying that onion growers had sat helplessly for five years while "unprincipled gamblers, who have not one cent invested in the production or distribution of the crop," ruined onion prices.

Michigan congressman Gerald Ford proposed a bill to ban onion futures trading. The Merc's president, E. B. Harris, fought off the bill, defending the exchange's turf as he spoke to the Senate Agriculture Committee in August 1957: "If there be abuses in [onion] futures trading, the Chicago Mercantile Exchange will be the first to condemn and help correct. . . . But we submit that burning down the barn to find a suspected rat is a pretty drastic remedy."

His speech fell short. In August 1958, President Eisenhower signed the Onion Futures Act. A proud Idaho representative told the National Onion Growers over a lunch shortly afterward that the ban had freed them "from the menace of onion futures trading."

On Franklin Street, the traders were annoyed. Some believed deep down that Piowaty was right about onions: They were condiments, not a food like eggs. As such, they weren't necessary in the way that foods were. The demand was more fickle. But losing the onion market cost money. Merc members lost brokerage customers, who had hired them to make trades in the onion pit. They lost the brokerage fees paid by traders who needed backing. They also lost whatever money they had hoped to make trading. And the seats, or memberships, they owned on the exchange all lost value too. Many vented to each other about Piowaty, who traded until the last day of the onion market.

The Merc tried to get the onion ban reversed by filing a lawsuit alleging that the ban restricted free trade, but the argument fell flat in federal court. A professor from Harvard advised the Merc's leaders to drop the fight. If they appealed to the U.S. Supreme Court and the justices ruled against the exchange, the decision could hurt the rest of the futures business. Besides, many onion growers now hated the traders. Without growers, and people who wanted to hedge, they didn't have a viable market. The traders dropped their court battle.

For a few months after the ban went into effect, the traders were distracted by a busy egg market. But when February rolled around, the trading floor got quiet. The members had little to do but make paper airplanes and play checkers. Some of the older members, after taking care of their Fulton Street businesses, spent hours in the break room playing gin rummy. Hi Henner's younger son, David, took a step further, leaving Chicago and the Merc for a new adventure in paradise. He leased his house and temporarily moved his family to Montego Bay, Jamaica, where he opened a nightclub.

Although members of the Merc now included a few onion dealers who had joined and set up clearing firms, it looked bad for the Merc, which needed to find something else to trade if it hoped to justify keeping the trading floor open. The governors of the Merc, inventive men, started thinking, and that's when the law of unintended consequences kicked in. In an attempt to contain the futures trade, Congress ended up unleashing it.

Pork Bellies   +0.05

In 1959, without onions to trade, the Chicago Mercantile Exchange seemed to have a bleak future. Bill Katz, the chairman, oversaw a depressed group of a dozen who sat on the board of governors. They periodically met around an oval table in a room just off the trading floor, next to the office of E. B. Harris, the powerful non-member president of the exchange. The Merc board operated like that of a condo association or a retirement village in Florida. When there was little important business to attend to, the meetings felt like a condo board fighting over pets, garbage pickup, or hallway temperature.

Members still came to the floor to trade futures on eggs and to dabble in futures on turkeys and potatoes. But the money the exchange brought in from trading fees didn't cover the cost of renting space on Franklin Street, paying the salaries of staff employees, and paying for other expenses such as linen towels for the washroom. Some members mentally prepared themselves to see their futures exchange fold. Of the 500 members, maybe 150 came to the floor before the onion debacle. Now even fewer bothered to show up.

Katz and the board of governors had been through tough times before. During the Second World War, trading dried up and the price of a membership fell to almost nothing. In dire straits, they sold the building to Henry Crown, a businessman who was using a building materials supply company to become one of the richest men in Chicago. But in general, when a pit got slow, the members opened another, diversifying as someone would in any business.

Members of the Merc needed another product to trade to replace onions. They needed a product that had prices that fluctuated, which would attract people in the business who wanted to hedge away risk as well as traders who wanted to speculate. To fit the mold of a typical commodity, it needed to be seasonal, storable, and gradable. The governors formed a committee and made one of their number, the broker Glenn Andersen, a talkative, medium-sized man with a slight paunch, its chairman. Sydney Maduff, a bifocals-wearing egg broker originally from Iowa, also joined the committee.

One of their ideas was to trade pork bellies. A pork belly is a slab of hog meat that, when cured, smoked, and sliced, becomes bacon. Some traders were familiar with pork bellies because they had been delivered to the cold storage warehouses, often frozen as a block, then chipped apart to be stored. Thanks to thousands of years of Jewish dietary law, some at the Merc knew little more than that about pork bellies, but they were not the types to let religion get in the way of business. According to one story, Hi Henner, when asked why he was trading on one of the holiest days of the Jewish calendar, took out a stack of bills and proclaimed that stack his god.

A few committee members went to Wisconsin and visited a pork-processing plant to learn the business and the hog industry lingo. Small farmers bred their sows to have babies in the spring and the fall. After about six months, these pigs were ready for market, so the farmers sent them to a stockyard and sold them. The hogs went to a packing plant owned by a company such as Armour or Patrick Cudahy, which was outside of Milwaukee. The packer killed the hog and separated out various parts for finicky customers. People in New England liked a "picnic," the front leg of a hog, while people in the Midwest preferred the "ham," the back leg. And everyone liked the bellies, which were turned into bacon.

The belly business had a seasonal price swing. Packing companies produced more pork bellies than they could use in the spring and fall, so they took them to a cold storage warehouse and froze them, dipping them twice in ice water to give them a double coating of ice to guard against freezer burn. Then the packers took them out when bellies were in short supply, in the summer, when tomatoes were in season and Americans wanted to eat bacon, lettuce, and tomato sandwiches.

The problem—and the reason a futures contract could work—was that the packer had risk. If prices went down while the pork bellies were frozen, he could get stuck with a bunch of frozen pork bellies that had lost value. It was critical for the packers to time the market correctly, and the risk was highest around Labor Day. Packers wanted bellies to sell to the rush of vacationers who returned home to empty refrigerators and loaded up on bacon, and they wanted bellies to sell immediately after that to mothers who served bacon to their children for the first few days of school. But after a few weeks, they typically told the kids to make their own breakfasts. And after that rush, if the packers had frozen inventory when the fall crop of bellies hit, they were stuck with them. At that point, the mantra in the business was to "sell it or smell it." But to Andersen, Maduff, Katz and the rest of the traders at the Merc, this seasonal problem created a trading opportunity.

There was some question as to what to name the new contract. The term "pork belly" sounded ridiculous, like something to tickle. But that was the term used by pork packers, and it was also a term sure to stick in a speculator's mind. So the Merc stuck with "pork bellies."

Besides the ticklish issue of the name, members hit another problem, one inside their building. The clearing firms had desks on the trading floor. Most of these firms were owned and run by men who got their start on Fulton Street, but a few big desks were run by the so-called wire houses—large brokerage firms with offices around the country where they lured in retail customers to trade stocks and, to a lesser extent, futures. The wire houses included the New York firms E. F. Hutton, Shearson Hammill, and Merrill Lynch. Each employed a man to work on the trading floor at the Merc. The Merc members believed they needed these wire houses and their customers to make a new market work, and the man who worked for Merrill Lynch vowed aloud to never have anything to do with pork bellies. The food business had some shysters, and the meat business may have seemed especially packed with people who cheated their customers and their suppliers with equal enthusiasm.

But the members went ahead anyhow. They opened a pit for pork belly trading in 1961. The egg dealer Ira Zeidman moved into the pit the first day. There was not much to do. A few orders came in, but not many. It looked like the pork belly trade was going to fail, and if it did, the Merc's prospects were not good. If that had happened, the story would end here.

Around the country a few people started trading pork bellies. Cattle buyers hung out during the winter in downtown El Paso, Texas, where the weather and drinking were good. When the calendar flipped to 1962, one buyer named Charlie Andrews, twenty-four years old, bought and sold cattle on behalf of people in the meat business. He heard about pork belly futures, looked up the nearest brokerage office, and walked into an E. F. Hutton office on the ground floor of a building downtown. He put $5,000 in an account and started trading pork bellies.

But there weren't many people like Charlie Andrews. So members of the Merc came up with still more ideas of commodities to trade. Cribbing an idea from some Harvard Business School professors, E. B. Harris suggested that the members trade futures on orange juice concentrate. The Merc's board members rejected the idea. That April members tried futures on frozen broilers—chickens raised for their meat—but that didn't work as well as hoped. Only a few companies dominated the business, and they had the power to move the market at will. When those companies met in the pit, their buying and selling ran roughshod over individual traders.

While the members looked for things to trade, a few people left. On the Monday after Easter, a popular sixty-two-year-old egg and onion trader from the West Side named Joseph Crilly died in the egg pit of a heart attack. A doctor—a member's son who was visiting his dad that morning—walked over and pronounced Crilly dead. The men around him stopped briefly, then began trading over him, shouting for someone to please come and take the body away. Crilly was Irish Catholic. He had by chance made his way to the Merc, but the rest of his family was at the Board of Trade, including his son Richard, who was a broker in the soybean pit and, in a stroke of luck, also a trained mortician. He ran over and took away his father's body, thus ensuring that no publicity was drawn to the exchange and, in line with the family's wishes, no autopsy was required. The other traders said that was the way to go, and E. B. Harris wrote a poem about Crilly as a eulogy. After disposing of the body, the younger Crilly had to come right back and sort out his father's positions to get out of the losers. He then bought his father's membership, although he remained a bean broker.

As members left, others came. A few women even joined. Later that year, John "Bud" McCarthy Jr., son of the butter trader John McCarthy, had wanted to start a clearing firm but needed a business partner with a membership—so he bought a membership for his wife, Nancy. At that time, women weren't allowed on the exchange floor during trading hours. At the Merc, any wives who wanted to meet their husbands for lunch waited in the hall, outside the double doors, until the closing bell. There was not even a women's restroom on the floor.

But the day Nancy McCarthy was approved for membership, Bud said that she should go on the trading floor. When they headed there, the guard stationed at the door was frantic and ran to E. B. Harris, who told him that Nancy was a member so it was fine to let her past. A few traders shot her dirty looks, but many of their friends ran up, shook her hand, and offered congratulations. For several weeks, she went daily to the building and answered phones at the company's desk on the trading floor. But she had four young children at home who needed her attention, so she left and planned to go back to the floor another time.

There would soon be female clerks, but the exchange remained a macho business. Wrote agriculture professor Thomas Hieronymus nine years later, in 1971, "Some houses refuse to accept the accounts of women. Whether this is because women complain so much when they lose that the business isn't worthwhile or whether they think that women are psychologically incapable of accepting the risks of commodity speculation is uncertain."

Barry Lind—a South Sider and the stepson of a radio personality named Phil Lind—also bought a membership to the Merc in 1962. His father and uncles had formed a trio and sung in some major nightclubs, but Barry did not have a gift for song. He was a young Woody Allen lookalike, with thick glasses, a slouch, and a knack for numbers. Lind had quit a job when he felt that his boss stiffed him out of a bonus, and he was casting about for a new job when he met Dave Becker's sons, Phil and Sam, at a party that Lind only went to because it happened to rain that day. They and his father lent him money to buy a membership. The young Lind hoped, ambitiously, to make $50,000 annually as a broker on the floor.

He ran a small advertisement in the Midwest edition of the *Wall Street Journal* to locate people interested in trading. In the ad, he called himself an egg specialist, and he might as well have strapped meat to his head and waited for the wolf, six-foot-tall Bill Henner. With people he liked, especially outside of market hours, Henner could be friendly and supportive. But in the pit, when the bell rang, a trader had no friends, especially him. Between his height, a slight limp due to childhood polio, and a booming voice, Henner had perfected the art of intimidation, which helped him get good prices for his trades.

Henner stopped Lind on the floor, stood in front of him, and demanded to know what made him such a specialist when members like Henner and his family had been there for years. Lind defended his ad and said that what he meant was that he specialized in eggs, not turkeys or anything else being traded. But it didn't matter. Lind made $3,200 that year, a far cry from what he'd hoped.

In 1963 trade hit a ten-year low. The Merc handled just 268,031 contracts, down from 416,156 the year before. To break out of the funk, the members tried trading shrimp—which seemed so promising that Gil Miller, head of the committee that recommended it, effused that shrimp was "mysterious, glamorous." He insisted that the vast number of shrimp in the sea would make the market presumably impossible to corner. That may have been true in theory, but it was false in practice. The Merc's contract called for sellers to deliver very high-quality frozen shrimp—of such high quality that the shrimp used in the shrimp cocktail at Chicago's fancy Drake Hotel would probably not have met the contract's exacting standards. On top of that, there was a rumor on the trading floor about a storm in the Gulf of Mexico that had supposedly disturbed the shrimp beds, and a rush of buyers bought up futures contracts. As a result, in the very first month that shrimp was to be delivered on the futures contract, sellers had trouble finding enough shrimp to deliver to buyers. The contract was revised, but it still died.

Then came January 1964. The Merc members, still desperate for a successful futures contract, launched a market for frozen hams. Lind dropped the specialist tag and made a cold call to the meatpacking company Swift and spoke to an executive, hoping to interest the company in hedging. The executive was interested, but not just in hedging the company's risk. Instead, he and other executives there realized that they could use what they knew about the hog market to make some extra money for themselves trading futures. Lind signed up the executive and some of his Swift colleagues as clients. His income jumped from $2,000 a month to $3,000 a week.

He also found well-off individuals, doctor and lawyer types who had some money to burn and might like bragging at cocktail parties about their commodities deals. Many stockbrokers offered futures, if at all, as an afterthought. Retail traders didn't use futures much, which was just as well because many might last a year before losing all the money they had put into futures trading. But while they were in the market, they were active customers. As his customers traded, Lind collected commissions for every "round turn"—a buy and sell.

The pork belly market did better that year. Lind had a steady and growing supply of customers. When some customers failed and stopped trading, he found more. There always seemed to be someone else who wanted to try trading pork bellies. Lind started making real money, $150,000 a year. He scraped together $50,000, which was what he needed then to open a clearing firm. His income went up even more.

Pork belly fever spread across the trading floor. On Fulton Street, some of the egg dealers had gotten into the pork belly business. They were buying bellies, storing them in warehouses, and selling the bellies for a profit at the Merc. Maduff had a desk near the door to the trading floor and often stood there, with both hands slid into the high belt of his trousers, palms down and thumbs out, like Fred Mertz, the landlord on *I Love Lucy*. He rocked rhythmically on his heels and made a point of talking to every person who came through.

Roy Simmons, one of the biggest traders on the floor, took delivery of a lot of pork bellies and asked Maurie Schneider to find someone to buy them. Schneider called around and found a buyer, the company Rath Packing, a pork packer out of Waterloo, Iowa. Then Schneider, too, started trading belly futures.

Before long, most of the egg traders preferred hanging out in the pork belly pit, as did some members who had taken a break from the floor. Leo Melamed was a chain-smoking, black-haired lawyer who had been a runner at the Merc during law school. He had bought a membership, then spent less time there after the onion debacle. But then he came back and traded part-time. Melamed was a fair trader, innocuous in the crowd. His face gave the impression that he was looking somewhere off in the distance, disconnected from the mayhem.

Six years after the collapse of onion trading, the Merc started to feel like it did back in the good old days. The pork belly market was more volatile than eggs or onions had ever been. It attracted a diverse group of people, including cab drivers, meat producers, and even some people in Hollywood. Word went around that John Wayne traded pork bellies, lost $1 million, and made a lousy picture because of it.

The pork belly future was ripe to squeeze and corner, to the horror of some and delight of others, and it was a perfect fit in the trading schedule. The egg trade wound down in January. The pork belly delivery season started in February and ended in August. The May pork belly contract was one of the busiest times, the halfway point. It was recorded on the blackboard as "PBK"—the "PB" stood for pork bellies, and "K" was futures shorthand for May. Ira Zeidman would eventually ditch the egg business and make enough in bellies to buy a Mercedes and later a boat, which he docked at Belmont Harbor on the north side of town and named *PBK*.

But that was still to come. In 1964, Bob Dylan was singing that the times were a-changin.' That year, Reverend Martin Luther King Jr. held a rally at Soldier Field, Chicago's football stadium, and Congress passed a civil rights bill outlawing discrimination. Meanwhile over on Franklin Street, the pork belly converts were rounding up customers to join them in delightful disrepute. Their voices bounced off the walls and ceiling. The Merc had turned a corner and was back in business.

Cattle   +0.06

Charlie Andrews, long before he donned a green suit and drove his Impala to Chicago, was practically born trading. While in grammar school in central Kansas, he traded goats for horses, and horses for cattle. By age twenty-four, he had crossed the central states a dozen times. He went to Mexico and bought thin cattle. He brought them back across the border and found buyers at the stockyard in El Paso. Some cattle companies started buying from him as his name got around. When the season ended in February, he visited cattle growers, then ranchers and the feedlots where cattle were sent to be plumped up. He drove 200,000 miles a year, often at night, when he could hit 110 miles an hour on the empty roads in his long and boxy Impala, with its chrome trim reflecting the moonlight.

Andrews visited other stockyards, also called terminal yards. He went to yards in Sioux City and Kansas City, swung through bigger yards in Omaha, and visited Chicago's Union Stock Yards, which stretched from Thirty-ninth to Forty-seventh Street, and from Halsted Street to Ashland Avenue. This was the famous square-mile city of animals on the South Side of Chicago.

The yards were anchored by the exchange building, a brick building that had a cafeteria and a saloon, complete with swinging doors and sawdust on the floor. Men tromped in with manure-covered boots. A man named Ray Spane came into the exchange building on a particularly cold day, was offered a cup of coffee to warm him up, and turned it down, saying, "Coffee, me arse, it's whiskey I need!"

It also had offices inside for several dozen commission firms. There brokers arranged deals between sellers and buyers who came from nearby or from packing companies in Michigan or on the East Coast. The dean of the brokers was a man named Dolan who had once employed a young man from a nearby neighborhood named Richard J. Daley. Daley went on to be mayor and never left the neighborhood.

The exchange building was surrounded by a sea of animals. On one side was Hog Alley, where large covered areas housed thousands of hogs. On another side, and even bigger, was Cattle Alley, with rows upon rows of square, wooden pens housing thousands of head of cattle. Smaller cattle came in from Colorado and Montana, shipped to Chicago before they could be covered in snow. Sometimes those cattle came accompanied by a cowboy in boots and a wide-brimmed hat who had instructions to keep the cattle in his sight until they were sold to feedlots. He slept near them, on a board, under the glowing Chicago sky. Heavier cattle came in from Iowa and neighboring states, after feeders fattened them up with corn to sell to packers.

Each commission firm had its own area of the yards, and buyers and sellers met between the pens and dickered over price. When they agreed on one, cowboys with canes pushed the cattle into alleys, sometimes onto elevated alleys that looked like platforms for Chicago's elevated trains, but with cattle chugging by instead.

The men moved the cattle to scales to be weighed. Then they drove some to loading docks to be put on trucks and sent to packing companies on the East Coast, and they drove other cattle through the alleys to another section of the yards called Packing Town. It looked like a small city of buildings hiding violence inside. They were owned by the meatpacking companies like Armour and Swift and were where, in efficient, assembly-line fashion, the hogs and cattle met their makers. The workers got a steer or heifer in, stunned it with what looked like a sledgehammer, hoisted it off the ground, cut the jugular, and let the blood run out. They separated the offal—the head, guts, hide, and hooves. The packer sold off what it could of that and put six hundred or so pounds of meat in a giant cooler. Some of the blood and guts ended up in a fork of the Chicago River, where it bubbled up and earned the name Bubbly Creek. Ultimately the meat ended up on tables as butt steaks and ground beef.

At the end of each day the yard workers kicked back. Cowboys in from western states ate at restaurants at the Stock Yard Inn next door. It was a three-story building modeled on an English Tudor mansion with two hundred dingy hotel rooms and some restaurants known for steak. The Sirloin Room had walls paneled with plywood, white tablecloths, worn carpeting, and upholstery. The Matador Room featured bullfighting paraphernalia in the wall cases. In 1964 it offered steak dinners from $5.25.

Hundreds of men working in the yards, most of them Irish, went to saloons. There was one in the back of the Stock Yard Inn, but there were plenty more on Halsted Street. The hog and cattle men generally drank separately, in part so they could insult each other in peace. The hog men smelled awful. The cattle men were rowdy and prone to fights. A smart man drinking with cattle men would take care, especially on St. Patrick's Day, when the bars got so packed they were dangerous. They became the kind of place where a man named Bud Doyle might hit a man named Barney Branigan with a pool cue.

But the whole business—the antics, characters, and alleys—was marked. Starting in the late 1950s, some buyers left for jobs out west because the market was moving in that direction. A packing company formed called the Iowa Beef Packers (IBP), and it built a super-efficient meatpacking plant, a factory that was bigger, newer, and fancier. It was able to handle the ever-larger herds of cattle coming in, and it handled them more cheaply. IBP built the plant closer to large feedlots because it made sense to keep the business in one area and to eliminate the cost of shipping cattle to Chicago and then farther east. Instead of shipping around live animals, they only shipped the beef.

This caused the biggest change in the stockyards since the days of Philip Armour and George Swift. The old plants couldn't compete with the newer, more efficient plant, so companies followed and copied IBP. They opened huge packing houses in Nebraska and other western states. Feedlots there got bigger. Companies started closing their packing houses in Chicago in the late 1950s and continued into the 1960s.

The market had long been made in the stockyard alleys of Chicago, and the price even went out on the radio. However ugly it actually was outside, a radio announcer would say it was a beautiful day in Chicago, then give the price of cattle. In the country farmers with some cattle out back listened and decided whether to ship the animals to the stockyards. But the new packing plants bought directly from the feedlots, and the feedlots bought cattle from growers. The new system was cheaper and efficient, and it eliminated the public market in Chicago.

Somehow or another, the egg and pork belly traders on the floor of the Chicago Mercantile Exchange took to the idea of trading cattle. None of them could tell a cow from a hog, but Glenn Andersen, the broker who pushed pork bellies, took a trip to Texas and learned about the business. They already traded pork bellies—how hard could this be?

Hard, it turned out. Cattle, unlike pork bellies, were alive. Commodities the traders dealt in were typically not walking around. That forced them to reevaluate and to figure out more precisely what made a futures contract work.

They had believed that a commodity needed to be seasonal. Prices fluctuated with the weather. But the cattle business wasn't seasonal, and prices still fluctuated. The cattle industry was prone to booms and busts, and the price changed with production. There were many people growing cattle, and they didn't coordinate with each other as they raised them and fattened them up. They often grew cattle and cut back at once. Because of that, the industry was like a pendulum swinging wildly: Sometimes there were too few cattle, and sometimes there were too many.

Typically, commodities in the futures business were also gradable. When a product was graded, both buyer and seller knew what kinds of eggs or bellies were changing hands. But it was trickier to grade cattle. It took a cattle buyer's eye. When making a deal, a buyer stood outside a pen in the yards and looked at a bunch of cattle. He looked for the right shape, the right heft, the right amount of whatever it was that hung under the throat of a steer. He wanted to see the things that told him the animal had the right amount of muscle and fat so that when it met its maker it would become a tasty, tender burger or steak. He knew exactly what he was looking for, but it was tough to describe it on paper.

And every other commodity traded with futures contracts could be stored. Grain could be kept in a grain elevator for a rainy day. Eggs were stuck in cold storage warehouses for a few months. Traders considered that important, in part because if a speculator took delivery of eggs, he had the option to store them for a month and sell them back into the market. That was part of the game they played. But traders couldn't store a herd of live animals for a month. The animals would need food and water. They might not survive. And moving them could be a royal pain.

At the Merc, some of the older egg men thought the idea of trading cattle was ridiculous, but they went ahead with it anyway as an experiment. They timed the launch in November 1964 to coincide with the Super Bowl of the cattle industry, the International Livestock Show. Held at the Chicago stockyards, the livestock show drew thousands of men, women, children, and, of course, animals. E. B. Harris managed to borrow one of the winners, a small, 420-pound, black Aberdeen Angus calf. On the day after Thanksgiving, he brought it to the trading floor on Franklin Street and paraded it in front of the chalkboard set up for the cattle trade. With that, the bell rang and a few men started trading a futures contract on live cattle. Andrews called in orders from the road.

Some Merc traders gave it a try, although young children on ranches knew more than these men. To learn to tell a cow from a steer and other basic information, they attended weekly lectures at the Chicago campus of the University of Illinois, where agriculture professors from Champaign came in to teach and no doubt chuckle at their students. Business was slow in the cattle pit. A few men in the cattle business were interested, but when they weren't around, members traded with each other, buying and selling to make it look like they were busy, hoping to attract attention and interest from potential customers.

A month after they started trading, they attracted the attention of the Board of Trade. The members of the large grain exchange rarely acknowledged that the Merc existed, but Board chairman Bernard Carey announced that the grain traders would also be going into the beef business. The Board members didn't consider the Merc much competition and launched their own live cattle contract, offering a potential one-stop shop for people in the cattle business. Some cattlemen traded corn futures because they used corn as feed, so they could stick around and hedge cattle at the Board of Trade too. At the Merc, Harris worried that the Board would kill the contract and accused the Board members of violating an unwritten law holding that the exchanges would not fight over a market.

A cattle buyer from the stockyards went to the Board. He found that it had Irishmen, just like in the stockyards. But by then, people in the cattle business had started trading at the Merc. Once a group of people had gathered in one place, it was hard to get them to move—like trying to get a large family to choose a restaurant. The Board eventually gave up on cattle, and the Merc expanded into trading other live animals, namely hogs.

Brokers were drumming up customers for the pork belly business, and some did the same for cattle futures. A man from the brokerage company Bache & Company visited a feedlot in Arizona, where he met and recruited a round-faced, personable, twenty-six-year-old worker from Indiana named Bob Rufenacht. When talking to someone new, Rufenacht easily adopted the cadence and accent of the person, from the twang of a Texan to the flat vowels of a Minnesotan. After moving to Chicago to start Bache's cattle futures department, he went to the pit, where there were just a handful of traders.

In 1966 a young man named Thomas Dittmer got a job as a runner. He was paid $82 a week to run orders into the pit so brokers could fill them. Dittmer was a second-generation Merc member. His stepfather, Ray E. Friedman, had a wholesale food business in Sioux City, Iowa. Friedman sold grade B chickens as grade A to the Army during the Korean War and went to jail for it, but came back with a presidential pardon and Dittmer in tow.

There were only three hundred men on the floor, seventy-five or so in the belly pit. They formed a curious crowd of men shouting out numbers, sometimes thumping each other on their chests and shoulders as they made deals. To build a brokerage business on the floor, Dittmer needed a membership. So lacking the money for a seat, he went "upstairs," the term for the offices off the trading floor. There he looked for customers outside the building who would be interested in trading cattle. On the advice of an egg broker in the office, he called every man and business related to feed, grain, or livestock in a fifty-mile radius. He went to a livestock show at the stockyards, set up a card table, and handed cattlemen his business card and Merc brochures.

Glenn Andersen and Bob Rufenacht also went to the stockyards. They met Glenn Bromagen, a Kentucky-raised cattle buyer who was in business for himself, buying and selling cattle on commission. He was interested in what they said about futures. Bromagen saw that business was slowing around the stockyards, so he and the Dolan brothers, sons of the biggest broker there, opened a futures office in the exchange building at the yards, and they talked up futures to the cattlemen coming through. In 1967 Bromagen left the stockyards, bought a membership, and moved to the Merc full-time. The traders called him "Rebel," a name he got at the yards thanks in part to his Kentucky accent. Rufenacht got him a trading badge that said "REB."

Around then, someone also brought in Harold Heinold, a big man in small Kouts, Indiana, thanks to his hog business. He had a black crew cut, a powder-blue suit, white socks and a white belt, and dozens of hog-buying stations throughout the Midwest. He also had a genuine, constant semi-grin. He figured that futures could be great for farmers and hog growers, and soon he had a clearing firm, Heinold Commodities. He had his hog market managers send possible futures traders his way. Then he set up commodity offices across the country, featuring price boards with lights and noises designed to entice people to trade. Farmers, among other people, walked in, sat down, and watched the prices of hogs, pork bellies, and grains fly by.

The meat pits also snared some people who knew nothing about that world, including a young man named Dick Dempsey, who was working for a stock brokerage that was bought by a company with a commodities arm. He could make good commissions with futures, so he found some customers, including one who owned two hundred acres in Zion, Illinois, and who bought some hog futures to speculate with. Dempsey's customer hoped the price of hogs would go up. Unfortunately for him, the price went down. Worse, he held on to the futures, hoping his luck would change.

As so often happens, it didn't. When the contracts expired, he still owned them and had to take delivery of a few thousand hogs. Dempsey got a call about it and went to investigate. He left his office on La Salle Street and got on a public bus heading south. The farther he went, the more he felt out of place as he crossed invisible borders that divided neighborhoods. Only a few months before, Martin Luther King Jr. had marched through a neighborhood near the yards calling for integration. The militant Black Panther Party was setting up on the West Side. After Dempsey transferred to a different bus, he was the only white person on it, and the only man in a suit and tie.

He could smell and hear the stockyards from blocks away. He got off the bus at Forty-third and Halsted and went to the exchange building, where a man looked at his dress shoes and handed Dempsey some boots. Then he led the broker through a maze of pens and pointed to some hogs, telling Dempsey that his customer owned them. He asked Dempsey if he wanted them fed and watered, which was called "yardage" and cost money. Dempsey said yes, then went back and explained the situation to his customer. A few days later, Dempsey made the trip again. His customer, it turned out, owned yet more hogs. Again, Dempsey met the charges and agreed to pay yardage. His customer was reluctant to admit defeat, but Dempsey arranged for him to sell all the hogs to Armour, at a loss. The hogs and the new speculator both got killed in the process. Dempsey bought a membership to the Merc a few years later.

The decade had started with the butter and egg men, led by Bill Katz in his trademark classy dark suit. After the onion trade died, he and Glenn Andersen and other board members saved the Merc. They remained in business, with most members still founders or sons of founders.

In 1965, even with the pork belly trade taking off, a group of younger members in their thirties and forties remained frustrated with the state of the exchange. They included Robert "Bob" O'Brien, the well-spoken son-in-law of butter dealer John McCarthy, as well as the broker Barry Lind and the lawyer Leo Melamed, who left his law practice to trade full-time. The group often ate together at the Bismarck Hotel and discussed the exchange. To be sure, they loved the growing excitement. In the pork belly pit, men lunged at each other to make trades, using hand signals to communicate in the din. But the younger men believed that the men still at the helm of the Merc were too set in their ways. They wanted to give the exchange a reputation they could be proud of rather than the one it had—that of being a bunch of crooks.

Had they held off, time and demographics would have been in their favor. But with war raging in Vietnam and hippies gathering in the streets, they were feeling more revolutionary than patient and respectful. They were also schooled in the tumultuous world of Chicago politics, defined by backroom dealings and swift political maneuvers. With some of that spirit, the younger group got a toehold on the board of governors in 1966 and gained control the next year. In 1967 they elected O'Brien chairman. He was a cross-roads candidate. He had connections to the older members and to the younger ones. Leo Melamed was secretary. He was politically ambitious and wrung his position for all it was worth, writing letters to members every time he could.

The next year, 1968, was one of the craziest the country had seen in decades. The killings, protests, and flower children that defined the year all showed up in Chicago. Martin Luther King Jr., who had moved into a West Side ghetto for part of 1966, was assassinated on April 4. That tore open a wound on the West Side. Buildings went up in flames, broken glass covered the streets, and Mayor Daley called President Lyndon Johnson to send in federal troops. Then, in Los Angeles, another shooter killed Robert Kennedy, who had hoped to be named the Democratic candidate for president at the convention to be held in Chicago that August. Instead, thousands of Democratic delegates convened at the International Amphitheater by the stockyards to nominate another presidential candidate, and thousands more people—hippies with beards, long hair, poetry, joints, and probably some LSD—held protests downtown against the war. Daley sent in cops with tear gas and more National Guard troops. In the amphitheater, antiwar senator Abraham Ribicoff from Connecticut decried the "Gestapo tactics on the streets of Chicago." Chicago's mayor responded by yelling back what some saw as "fucker," although his supporters insisted he said "faker." His political machine survived the year, but new blocs of Republican voters sent Richard Nixon to the White House.

During this turmoil, Merc men were holed up in their enclave. Dittmer got his membership in 1968. His first day trading, he accidentally bought twenty egg contracts—and accidentally made $100,000 on them. Later on, he tried to buy five hundred egg contracts but didn't realize he was standing in the potato pit. The other traders were nice enough to sell the contracts back to him, but they made fun of him for it. The danger outside the building affected most of the members marginally. One member, to be on the safe side, sat by the aisle, not the window, on his train ride home each afternoon in case a rock came through the window. Another man on the trading floor believed the antiwar protestors were mainly interested in getting laid. Gil Miller's twenty-two-year-old son Alan was too busy to join the protest movement. He stayed late each night processing a flood of pork belly trades with pencils and punch cards as firms were just starting to use electronics to do the job.

A quieter kind of revolution was in the air at the Merc. Melamed was voted chairman in January 1969. Fewer people noticed or cared about this political handover, and the ones who did care tended to work on Fulton Street. Melamed professed great plans for the Merc. A few weeks after his election, he wrote a letter to the members and referred to "the immense future potential of our Exchange." It took some self-delusion to believe, as he professed to, that the exchange had "national prominence" and would have more in the years to come. But he was caught up in a patriotic spirit—or knew how to marshal it.

Merc members were also in a hopeful mood. In 1969, fully rehabilitated from his chicken debacle, Ray E. Friedman opened Ray E. Friedman and Company, or Refco for short, with his stepson Dittmer, who had been building a brokerage business for Gil Miller. That same year, Bromagen and Rufenacht started a clearing firm, teaming up with a cattle feeder named Fred Hertz who worked from St. Joseph, Missouri, an hour's car ride north of Kansas City. He became a huge trader and came to Chicago every so often to sample the saloons and a few pretty girls. They called their clearing firm Rufenacht, Bromagen & Hertz, or RB&H.

They all reached out to packers, feeders, and ranchers. Some might have thought that ranchers would like the idea of using futures conservatively, as insurance. Instead, ranchers became some of the riskiest speculators at the exchange. They tended to speculate with futures rather than use them to hedge, doubling down on the bet they were already making with their livelihoods. If cattle prices went up, that was good for their ranch, and it became good for their futures account too. If cattle prices went down, though, they were hurt on the ranch—and they lost money in futures. But ranchers were some of the country's most eager gamblers. Legend had it that one large ranch in Texas was named 6666 in honor of the poker hand the owner held that won him the ranch. Cowboys were optimistic to the core. The traders at the Merc started saying that the ranchers who doubled down with futures were putting on "the Texas hedge."

Soon the members could look out at the trading floor and see the makings of a meal. There was the egg pit, which was dying as the industry consolidated and growers tricked chickens with lights and heat into laying eggs all year. There was a pit for Idaho potatoes—a small market—and a pit for lumber. There was a pit for boneless beef, used for hamburgers. But the big pits were for cattle and—still the king—pork bellies.

It was a boys' club, and getting younger by the minute. The meat pits were full of men in their thirties suddenly making money. They used it to acquire things, whatever money could buy. Some bought toupees. More than one bald man came in having grown a full head of hair overnight. Some bought art and cars. They bought Rolex President watches—solid gold and a key to a better table at a restaurant. Almost all Merc men wore some version of the watch, some encrusted with diamonds. The Becker brothers, Sam and Phil, had a chauffeur named Otis who dropped them off in front of the building. And traders used money to acquire women, including some brave, pretty young things who'd started working as clerks on the trading floor. Traders went hunting for girlfriends and mistresses and wives.

Andrews stopped in at the trading floor regularly when he came through town. He traded cattle futures, a customer of RB&H. In 1970 he met a young woman, a phone clerk on the floor working for RB&H. He quickly proposed. They got married in Las Vegas, although she insisted they wait at least a little bit, until a lull in business in the cattle pit. Then she moved to Kansas with him.

A short time later, John "Jack" Sandner showed up. He was an Italian-Irish defense lawyer from the South Side who toyed briefly at age thirteen with becoming a priest but changed his course and became a local featherweight boxing champion while in high school. He went off to college, switched to wrestling, and became a lawyer, graduating with the Dean's Award from Notre Dame Law. Then he met E. B. Harris, who invited him to a Christmas party at Dellsher, Melamed's office. When some traders there asked why an outsider was at the party and pushed him out the door, Sandner, at his best when backed into a corner, responded by using his boxing skills in what he said was self-defense. In the hallway outside the office, he slapped one member and gave a right cross to another that knocked him unconscious. Sandner was eventually, after a fight, approved for membership to the increasingly boisterous club.

Consolidation changed the food business and Chicago. A West Side neighborhood deli named Dominick's was run by a father and son who organized sales on certain items faster than anyone else. Housewives started going there to find deals, and the family turned the deli into a chain of stores. A small company called Jewel Tea, which delivered tea and coffee, bought up grocery stores and also created a chain. The days of spending an afternoon going to the butcher and the vegetable stand and the mom-and-pop grocer drew to a close. Shoppers went simply to the chain stores, which got so big that smaller suppliers couldn't handle the business. The chains leaned on a few suppliers, which grew too as a result. They built long, low warehouses where they could find space. Some smaller suppliers, including egg and butter dealers, closed their shops on Fulton Street.

In 1971 the stockyards in Chicago closed. One hundred and six years after Old Hutch, Philip Armour, and other Board of Trade men opened businesses there, a bulldozer razed the pens and souvenir hunters snatched brass latches from gates. Two people tried to walk off with a bronze bust of Abraham Lincoln that once stood in front of the exchange building. Liquor warehouses moved in. A box factory had already opened in an old Swift meat-packing plant. The Stock Yard Inn was left behind, although it would be demolished a few years later. One of the few remnants to survive was a castlelike limestone gate that arched over the road to Packing Town.

With that, one of the last physical ties to the old frontier days disappeared. The men with whips and cowboy boots found other work. The Wild West was no match for corporate consolidation. As much as the frontier existed anywhere in the United States, it lived on in the small cattle pit at the Merc.

PART II

Currencies +0.07

When the stockyards closed in 1971, Chicago became just another big city with big-city problems. The frontier of the past was gone. But a new set of explorers came to town.

One came to Roosevelt Road. That was the name for Twelfth Street, which ran east-west a mile south of the city's Mason-Dixon line. Roosevelt started a few steps from Lake Michigan, formed the southern boundary of Grant Park, and passed Maxwell Street, which had once been full of pushcarts. A few miles farther out, Roosevelt turned into a commercial thoroughfare in a neighborhood known as Lawndale. Before the Second World War, that was Chicago's most Jewish neighborhood, packed with dozens of synagogues, two- and three-flat apartment buildings, and families just arrived from Maxwell Street and eastern Europe.

On Roosevelt Road before the Second World War, at the corner of St. Louis Avenue, people dragged out soapboxes and got up on them to preach about Zionism, communism, atheism, Judaism, socialism, and other -isms. Sometimes people heckled the outdoor orators or threw punches. When Leibl Melamdovich moved to town in 1941, the preachers were scattering, but their passion permeated the community. He was just a kid, having been shepherded by his parents out of increasingly dangerous Bialystock, Poland, through Siberia and Japan, then on to Chicago. Jews were beginning to migrate northward, and Melamdovich's parents took a third-floor walk-up apartment in a Northwest Side neighborhood called Humboldt Park, a neighborhood of Italians, Poles, and Jews.

The view that shaped his world was his parents' Bundism. His parents leaned socialist and spoke Yiddish, and they imbued in him a sense of purpose and mission.

Leibl Melamdovich later changed his name to Leo Melamed, which sounded more American. Besides Bundism, Melamed learned a flair for the dramatic. He recited Yiddish poetry to guests at home and at theaters two neighborhoods over in Lawndale. In high school, he starred in a play in the role of a young man in love with a tailor's daughter. The stage was set to resemble a room in the tailor's house, and Melamed's character was there talking to his beloved, although the two weren't supposed to be alone together. Melamed's job in one scene was to hear the tailor coming and leap through the open window. Instead, he heard the tailor, tried to leap, and got his left foot caught in the window. He brought the wall of the set down, and the audience too. The curtain quickly came down. That is the story he later recounted, and he told it so well that you couldn't help but wonder later if it really happened or if Melamed merely told a great story. But even if the story was more fiction than truth, it showed that something in Melamed's past taught him to love and work a crowd.

He considered making acting his career, but it became just a hobby. Instead, Melamed got jobs that paid, like driving a cab, working at the Montgomery Ward catalog warehouse, being a stock clerk at Marshall Field's, and teaching woodworking to Jewish children. Then he became a lawyer, a variation of an ambulance chaser. He exchanged tips with cops. When cops knew of accidents and people who might require legal representation, some let Melamed know, and he thanked them with a few bills. He also handled divorces and bankruptcies.

While he was in law school, his worldview and sense of purpose changed. He embraced capitalism and the idea of private ownership. He also found the Merc. As Melamed told the story, he had a job at a law firm but called in sick to work one day to go to the North Avenue beach and enjoy the sun and girls. He was caught by his immediate boss and fired. Then he needed another job and thought he was applying for a job at a law firm named Merrill Lynch, Pierce, Fenner & Beane. When he showed up to the interview, he was puzzled as to why it was in the Chicago Board of Trade building, and he was more puzzled when the employment officer sent him to 110 North Franklin Street, where he discovered that Merrill Lynch was a brokerage firm, not a law firm. He fell in love with the trading floor, darting in and out of the egg pit, getting kicked by some surly dealers.

Melamed bought a membership in 1954. His father was bothered by his son's blatantly capitalist behavior, but lent him money for it anyway when Melamed promised to finish law school and become a lawyer. Melamed was at the Merc when the onion trade died in 1958, and he was there when the pork belly trade started in 1961. He had a law practice with a partner, Maury Kravitz, the son of a Yiddish newspaper editor and a trim man at the time. Melamed and Kravitz purchased a boat they named *Dellsher*, a combination of the names of their children, Idelle and Sheryl.

The pork belly trade took off, and Melamed spent more time at the Merc. Kravitz took the law practice. Melamed took the boat and the name Dellsher, and in 1965 he opened a clearing firm with that name. Then he fell into the Merc like someone else might fall into a pleasant dream. It was a perfect fit. He was an actor, and the pits were his stage. A trader could be quiet and meek at home, but in the pit, when the market was open, he could be anyone he wanted. It was liberating. The niceties of polite society were forgotten. The trading room even had a gallery for him to play to.

The Merc's young, revolutionary posse provided him with a role. With this group, he could be a politician roiling up a crowd, a role he'd have trouble playing outside of the Merc. It had been twenty years since Lawndale's Jewish alderman, Jacob Arvey, did such a good job of getting out the vote for the Democratic Party that he'd been made chairman of the Cook County Democratic Committee, a high rank in the city's political machine. But in general, Chicago was a city where politicians were Irish, especially mayors. In many circles in the city Melamed was considered too Jewish to be elected to that office. The Merc became his city instead, and its members became his voting bloc.

When he became chairman in 1969, Melamed was focused on the futures business above all else and on reeling in speculators. Melamed invited a pack of journalists to the Merc and showed off the trading floor. They left with a sense of excitement that they fed to their readers. After listening to Melamed, it was hard not to want to rush right out and try trading, even having just been fully warned of the dangers.

In late 1969, figuring an economist might be useful, the crew at the Merc hired Mark Powers, a onetime farm boy from Wisconsin who wrote his doctoral thesis about pork belly futures. Soon after, the Merc men toed the line of a new frontier.

Eight hundred miles away from Chicago, at the tip of lower Manhattan, sat a small stone building across from Battery Park. It housed close to five hundred members of the New York Produce Exchange. It was one of several member-owned commodity exchanges in the neighborhood, one of the handful where people had started trading futures after the business developed in Chicago. The exchange had a few markets, but the biggest one was in cottonseed oil. That kept the traders busy most mornings, although many had other jobs in the afternoons. One was Murray Borowitz, who ran a trucking company when not on the floor. He was elected a director of the produce exchange in 1968.

The produce exchange was a few blocks south of Wall Street, the most famous financial district in the country, if not the world. There the powerful New York Stock Exchange had a near monopoly on the trade of American stocks. The blocks around the exchange held offices with people engaged in the business of stocks, bonds, foreign exchange, and all other things financial.

A block south of the produce exchange was New York Harbor. Water from the Atlantic Ocean cyclically mixed with the Hudson and East Rivers, swirling around Staten Island, Ellis Island, and the Statue of Liberty. Behind her, in New Jersey on the other side of the bay, was Allied Crude Vegetable Oil Refining Corporation, run by Anthony "Tino" DeAngelis.

DeAngelis was a five-foot-five man from the Bronx who became a butcher, then bought a controlling interest in a New Jersey meat company. He sold uninspected meat to the federal school lunch program and ended up in bankruptcy. He went on to allegedly sell inferior lard to the German government. Then, in 1955, he set up Allied Crude Vegetable Oil Refining in a two-story Bayonne building between some smelly petroleum storage tanks that he cleaned up for storing vegetable oil. He did brisk business in the Food For Peace program, a government-subsidized program in which U.S. companies sold surplus farm products to developing nations.

DeAngelis paid high prices for crude vegetable oil and sold refined oil for cheap. How he made money mystified competitors. It had to do with futures. He told customers he kept large amounts of oil in those tanks in Bayonne, New Jersey, and that included soybean oil and cottonseed oil. As a businessman with a large amount of product, he wanted to make sure it didn't lose value while it hung out in his tanks. So he traded futures. Many companies in his position hedged, trading futures simply to avoid losses. But in fact, for many companies the futures market proved a giant temptation to speculate. They used what they knew about the market to make some extra profit.

DeAngelis traded futures on soybean oil at the Chicago Board of Trade, and he traded futures on cottonseed oil at the New York Produce Exchange. He used the oil in the tanks as collateral to get bank loans, which he used to trade. But DeAngelis attempted a caper. He claimed to have 1.8 billion pounds of oil he didn't have. He tricked inspectors by floating oil on top of saltwater, which was available for free at the end of the dock. The ruse made it look like he had full tanks of oil, and he used all that phantom oil to buy so many futures that he seemed on his way to cornering the oil markets.

The scam unraveled on November 15, 1963. DeAngelis's company filed a petition for bankruptcy on November 19. In Chicago, inside the Board of Trade building, the trading floor turned into a mass of activity after the scandal erupted. For several hours, the floor was insanity, although there was order to the insanity. The chairman was Bernard Carey, a second-generation trader, and he insisted the market would sort out the mess. It was busy for several days as DeAngelis's brokers sold seventeen thousand contracts for whatever prices they could get. By the end of the week, the traders were exhausted. Then that Friday, November 22, President John F. Kennedy was assassinated. The traders were shocked, and the markets went crazy again. DeAngelis's scam created losses of $200 million and became known as the greatest financial swindle of the time. The Chicago Board of Trade expelled him as a member that December, then continued on with business.

But in New York, the trading floor in lower Manhattan was different. It went quiet. The members of the produce exchange voted to halt trading in cottonseed oil futures and sell contracts at arbitrary prices. When they stopped the market that day, that was it. Customers never came back to it in the numbers they did before.

The New York traders, left with less to do, were in the same desperate situation that Chicago's egg traders had been in after their onion scandal. Borowitz figured that they needed to launch another market, and he looked around for inspiration. He made two radical suggestions—both combined the futures business with the local specialty, the business of money. His first idea was to create a futures contract on stocks as a way to engage millions of people who owned stocks and might want to speculate or protect themselves from a market crash. That idea got nixed by regulators who perhaps did not want speculators mucking around in the stock markets. His second idea was to write a futures contract for foreign currencies.

It sounded bizarre to people in the food business, but Borowitz thought it could work. Currency rates didn't fluctuate much, but they did fluctuate. If an American thought the dollar was going to lose value, he could deposit money in a foreign bank or change money at a small foreign exchange dealer, but costs were often high. With futures, he could hedge or speculate with less cost and hassle.

The cottonseed oil traders got into the spirit of it. They formed an entity called the International Commercial Exchange, gave all the members a seat on it, and elected Borowitz its first president. One of the exchange's staff members set up a clearinghouse. They set up trading and launched in April 1970. Traders could buy and sell futures contracts for British pounds, French and Swiss francs, West German deutschemarks, Italian lira, and Japanese yen. Buyers who held on to the contracts could take delivery of the foreign money.

At first, there was trading. After a few months, however, and some difficulty securing Japanese yen to deliver, potential customers outside the building lost interest. The exchange members tried other things. They began trading pork bellies in 1971, saying their contract would be better than Chicago's for small and midsized hog slaughterers, but it didn't work. Borowitz died in February 1973. Three months later, in May, the produce exchange was dissolved and converted into a real estate trust owning just the historic building and the land it sat on. Ownership was divvied up among the 473 members, and the exchange was disbanded. The currency exchange was rolled into a neighboring exchange that dealt primarily in potatoes. Borowitz became the man behind one more failed futures market.

After Borowitz had launched his market, the Merc opened a similar one. The people in Chicago maintained that they came up with the idea independently, although who thought of it first is lost to history. By some accounts, when Powers interviewed for his job as the Merc economist, he suggested to E. B. Harris that the Merc launch a futures contract on foreign currencies. He discussed it with a foreign exchange dealer and studied the nuances of trading currencies.

Melamed said that he came up with the idea. He believed it was such a good one that someone else was sure to have it. When he heard that someone did, in New York, he and Harris stopped by and were relieved to find the trading floor as quiet as a library. Melamed said he felt the idea was still viable. The produce traders had made a mistake and simply thought too small. They had created a glorified currency exchange, which was fine for tourists planning a long trip to Europe, but Melamed said that he envisioned something bigger—a market for international commerce and involving far larger amounts of money. What he saw, he would say, was that the world was integrating, becoming a business melting pot.

The issue of who thought of what, when, could keep a top spinning for years. One person recalled Melamed being less involved at the start, and some shrugged and said Melamed tended over the years to rewrite details in stories to give himself the starring role. He, in turn, said that everyone wanted to take credit for a good idea. In the end it didn't matter who had the idea first, or how exactly it came about. Karl Benz invented the modern car, but Henry Ford figured out how to sell millions of Model Ts.

For decades, the dollar had been stable. By design, its value remained essentially the same relative to other currencies. Every year central bankers from around the world got together and decided what each of their currencies was worth. They pegged currencies to the dollar, and the Americans pegged the dollar to gold, saying that $35 could buy an ounce of gold. When individuals swapped money at currency exchanges, or companies swapped money through foreign exchange dealers at banks, they usually did so at close to the official rate. This was the Bretton Woods system, named for the town in New Hampshire where ministers gathered in July 1944 to set up rules for the new global economic order.

But sometimes they swapped money at a rate that differed from the official one—for example, if a company executive thought a country's economy and therefore its currency looked weak. Some people did this using forward contracts, speculating that central bankers would be forced to adjust the fixed exchange rate to something more realistic, which they often did. In the years after the Second World War, the market deviated more and more from the official exchange rates. It got harder for bankers to keep them fixed.

And exchange rates were becoming more important to millions of people. Just as the fur traders had pushed into the American West, in 1970 American businesspeople were pushing into other countries, finding suppliers and customers all over the world. Americans were falling in love with Japanese cars and Swiss watches. That meant the men and women doing business in Japan, Switzerland, and elsewhere had to exchange money. It was getting tough for them to budget because they didn't know how far the dollar would go in the near future.

If the futures men in Chicago didn't see in 1970 what was happening, they saw it a year later. In August 1971, President Richard Nixon tore up the Bretton Woods system. He announced that the country was not going to sell any more of its gold. From that moment on, the dollar was just a piece of paper. Its value would be set by the market and its rate allowed to "float." A few American tourists in Europe had trouble exchanging money because banks were temporarily unsure of what it was worth. Quickly the market started establishing exchange rates.

But there was no central market. If all the people exchanging money with forward contracts could get together in one place and make their deals in a public forum, then everyone would know the future exchange rates and could plan accordingly. And they could do that in Chicago, where Fulton Street egg dealers had already demonstrated their ability to trade other things—things they knew nothing about. Melamed and his associates decided to set up a new exchange and to give it a name free of any association with pork bellies or onions. Melamed selected the International Monetary Market, the IMM, which sounded grand.

To bolster their credentials, he contacted Milton Friedman, a University of Chicago economist who was already famous for his view that markets should operate without government intervention. There was a story floating around that Friedman had tried to sell British pounds, believing they were going to lose value, but that Chicago's big banks turned him away, saying that their markets were for companies only, not individuals. Three weeks later, the currency was devalued, and he could have made a profit. Harris and Melamed met Friedman in the Waldorf Astoria Hotel in New York and explained that they wanted to create a market in which individuals like himself would be free to speculate. He agreed to write a paper supporting the idea. He called it "The Need for Futures Markets in Currencies."

Melamed went to the Merc board of governors to explain what was in the works—a new exchange geared to futures on financial instruments. Although new, it would be in the same building, use the same chalk, and involve mostly the same staff people, like Harris and Powers. This idea didn't go over well with the older crowd at the exchange. Most of the older butter and egg men thought it was ridiculous. Their little club was busy enough already without going into financial markets. They had been a market for egg dealers but now shared the floor with hog brokers and cattlemen from the stockyards. The price of a membership to the exchange was up, and many were collecting loads of brokerage fees. But opening another pit, much less another exchange, could take people out of the pork belly and cattle pits, and business there could suffer. They didn't care what Milton Friedman said unless he ran a business on Fulton Street. They knew nothing about currency trading and paid little attention to currency rates, trade balances, or the speeches made by finance ministers.

And on a personal level, some just didn't like Melamed. Some people, particularly members who had been around the exchange for a while, viewed him as cocky. At board meetings, he was in the early stages of perfecting his powers of persuasion there. For years after, he used melodrama to get his point across. When speaking, he often paused for dramatic effect. Other times he took a lukewarm position on the topic at hand, then changed his mind at the last critical moment, masterfully bringing detractors along with him. If he mispronounced anything, like saying "grandoyze" instead of "grandiose"—which he was—no one in the room dared smirk. One man who *did* dare smirk quickly wiped that from his face. He realized that if Melamed saw it, he would remember it and not appreciate the humor.

But the butter and egg dealers were losing numbers. After O'Brien and then Melamed took over, some died, some retired, and some moved to offices. Miles Friedman, known for having a carnation in his lapel, had taken his business upstairs to an office and passed away that year at age eighty-eight. Some of the other old guard members were aging and passing on. Melamed had support among the younger members, including O'Brien, the former chairman, and Barry Lind, the onetime egg "specialist" who had reached and blasted past his goal of making $50,000 a year.

And Melamed could be very persuasive, especially when addressing a group and with heady dramatic material. He made currency trading seem like the Merc's destiny. In his story, the butter and egg men were heroes standing up for free markets and facing down oppressors. He promised a rousing conclusion, where independence and freedom would prevail.

So the idea of a new exchange cleared the board and went to a member vote. When Melamed said that every member of the Merc would get a membership to the new exchange for nothing, or close to it, he won over more detractors. Under his plan, they could remain in their respective pits and make some additional money by selling their seats after a year to anyone presumably ridiculous enough to want to trade currencies. With tepid enthusiasm, they voted to form the new exchange. One egg man, Isadore "Izzy" Mulmat, who ran Mulmat Brothers commodity brokers, refused to pay the $100 processing fee to get his otherwise free membership.

The exchange was new in name only. Almost everything else about it looked like the Merc. They made room for the monetary market in some unused space on the trading floor. They set up a single pit and hung 28 chalkboards on the walls, enough to trade seven currencies on a quarterly basis. They sold 150 more memberships for $10,000 apiece to raise money. They sold some to clerks who couldn't afford the increasingly expensive Merc membership. They even sold some to members of the Board of Trade, including Eddie and Billy O'Connor, as an investment.

The monetary market set up a board. To be modern, they called board members directors, not governors. At the Merc, where Melamed was subject to term limits as chairman, he passed that title to Michael Weinberg Jr., a man liked by old and young members alike. Melamed became chairman of the new exchange, which had no term limits. He wasn't about to introduce them. Once he had tasted power and success, he loved it and didn't want to give it up.

A few weeks before the launch, the soon-to-be market held a symposium. Everyone was surprised when more than seven hundred people showed up, including bankers and people from all over the world. They held a debate. The exchange staffers circulated Milton Friedman's paper in which he argued that a market like this was going to develop, so it might as well be in the United States. But another famous economist, recent Nobel Prize winner Paul Samuelson—the author of the most frequently assigned economics textbook of all time—criticized the idea. He questioned whether speculators should be involved, saying that "the thought of a growing army of uninformed amateurs getting their kicks" in foreign exchange was not reassuring, and he even brought up the onion futures market, a sore point to some audience members.

Perhaps Melamed really had been committed to the idea from the very start. But if he hadn't been—and some later expressed doubt—it's also possible that this symposium energized and focused him. He worshiped Milton Friedman, and hundreds of people had traveled to Chicago and gathered just to discuss this little exchange. Saying that he hadn't expected Samuelson to insult it, he became determined to make it work.

He got his chance when the monetary market opened in May 1972, steps from the cattle pit. The executive director of the International Monetary Fund spoke. Melamed, dressed in a snazzy striped suit, cut a ceremonial ribbon.

The Merc men had a habit of having women on hand when they launched a new market, ostensibly to get press coverage and a photo in the paper, not just to get men on the floor to turn their heads and pay attention for a few minutes. When they launched a market in Idaho potatoes, they had Miss Idaho visit the floor, dressed in a potato sack dress stitched together by the sister of Ron Frost, the exchange's public relations man. When they launched a market for frozen boneless beef, they had a young woman who worked on the floor, and who also modeled, ring the bell. Now, to launch currencies, they brought out a group of women wearing outfits from countries around the world. To launch the market in Japanese yen, for example, they pointed to a woman wearing a kimono.

It was good theater, but a bit ridiculous and hokey. It was also out of synch with the financial world that Melamed wanted so badly to conquer. The day the new exchange launched, a currency dealer at an unidentified New York bank made his disdain clear on the front page of the *Wall Street Journal*: "I'm amazed," he said, "that a bunch of crapshooters in pork bellies have the temerity to think that they can beat some of the world's most sophisticated traders at their own game."

Actually, few at the Merc really wanted to try to beat the currency traders at their own game. They included a bunch of guys who had just found out that pork bellies were bacon, and they were perfectly happy trading that. Melamed pressured some into trying currencies. After the New York banker's rude dismissal, Melamed appealed to their sense of pride and played the New York–Chicago card. They needed to show up the snobs in New York.

The exchange had traders sign a clipboard, getting five people to trade every half-hour. The traders' commitment was broadcast, posted on a wall in the hallway for everyone to see. If no customer sent in business, they traded with each other.

After the first few weeks, the pit had three eager young traders in it, waiting for some action. One was a woman, the first female trader at Franklin Street, Carol "Mickey" Norton, who had played bridge with Melamed and purchased a membership to the new exchange after he kept insisting she give trading a try. A few Merc members from the other pits, including Lenny Feldman, who had owned Whisky-a-Go-Go, a nightclub on Rush Street, joined them when other markets were closed.

Usually, the traders had little to do. There wasn't enough volume for them to make money by scalping (buying and selling quickly). Norton did the alternative: make longer-term, potentially risky bets about whether the market would go up or down. She could make a lot of money quickly, but she could lose as much just as fast. And who knew all the details of what made currencies move one way or another?

She didn't realize that the pit was like a loose wheel hanging off the side of the banking market—or even that the banking market existed. The traders quoted prices in the pit, but bankers quoted very different prices in their offices. The traders in the pit seemed disconnected from the business, and in fact they were. For their business to work, they needed to link the markets. Harris and Melamed hoped that the bankers would see an opportunity to make easy money. The pit was like a candy store for them. All they needed to do was, for example, use forward contracts to buy British pounds from one of their customers, then turn around and sell an equivalent amount of futures on British pounds for more money in the pit. It was a strategy in the business and called arbitrage, or "arbing." If they could do both trades quickly, they could lock in a quick profit and practically mint money. But the bankers lacked the risk-taking soul of traders using their own money. The bankers traded only a tiny amount of futures, if they traded at all.

Although the bankers weren't going to take advantage of price differences by arbing, a trader might do it—if only the banks would let them trade. Banks hadn't let Milton Friedman trade with them, and they weren't about to let these yokels trade either. But when pressed, Chicago banks were persuaded, because they made money off the futures business and competed with each other to do so, so they were willing to entertain the thought of allowing certain qualified futures traders to arbitrage between the pit and the bankers' private markets. Melamed created a class of membership to the exchange that eliminated the risk for the bank. Members who signed up for these "Class B" memberships could do only this type of trade.

So some traders signed up, including three brothers from the meat pits. One often stood at a desk near the pit with an ear on the telephone and eyes on the blackboard. The brothers would make enough trading currencies to build a fancy office complete with a steam room. Norton's husband also came to the floor, learned what to do, and split profits with Melamed. By arbitraging, they could make $100 or $1,000 on a trade, a few thousand dollars a day, practically risk-free. Eventually the bankers would realize how easy it was to make this money and they would instruct their men on the floor to trade.

In the meantime, a few months after the market launched, Melamed took his band on tour. Melamed, Harris, Mark Powers, Barry Lind, and several other members went to Europe to introduce themselves to central bankers, dressed in smart suits paid for with the growing riches created by the pork belly, hog, and cattle trade. They had short and sweet meetings with the bemused bankers whose currencies they wanted to trade. They met with bankers at the Bank of England who, when the Americans were leaving, politely asked to let them know if there was anything they could do to help. One of the Chicagoans—and Melamed said it was him—less politely and as a joke, suggested that they float the British pound. That way, traders in the market, not the bankers, would set the currency rate. In Italy the next morning they picked up the paper and saw that the Bank of England had floated the pound. They gathered in a café in Rome to discuss the effects and figure it out. "What does that mean, float the pound?" asked one of the directors.

Before they headed home, Lind went shopping for a suit. He had made enough in the prior decade to buy the finest, so he went to the shop Brioni on Via Barberini, where there was an old tailor behind the counter who he was sure was the owner. He bought several suits and shirts and paid with an American Express card. When he got home, he studied a bill for $1,725, like a college student who had just taken Economics 101. Curious about the exchange rate he had paid, he told his assistant to find out what the Italian lira had traded for in the pit on that day. Based on what she found out, he figured that American Express had bilked him out of $25. He called American Express and exchanged some letters with the company. Then someone at American Express, fed up with the correspondence, canceled his card. Lind had to humble himself to get it back. The experience made him confident—even more than before—that currency futures would work. The traders in the pit offered better deals than the banks were willing to give.

The pork belly pit was still the most active on the floor, full of young, aggressive men. Some were members' sons, but some, like Harry Lowrance, were outsiders working their way up from not much. Lowrance had started working for the exchange in his teens, not long after getting caught taking a joyride in a car that one of his neighbors stole. He later worked for Heinold, who in 1970 lent him the money to buy a membership. Lowrance became known as Harry the Hat, thanks to a memorable fluorescent orange number he once wore. He went into the belly pit wearing a red trading jacket, which many traders wore, but also colorful bellbottoms and platform shoes. Then he started wearing velvet pants and a fur coat. He became known as a daredevil driver. He joined other traders to drink on Rush Street, but even when he was sober, a passenger had to think twice before getting into his vehicle.

The day the new exchange started, a Greek kid named James "Jimmy" Kaulentis joined the belly pit. Having grown up by Wrigley

Field, he knew no one on Fulton Street. But he got interested in the Merc when he was working in a training program to become a stockbroker, asked for a $50 raise, and got turned down. A friend told him he could make $200 a day at the Merc, which he didn't believe but went anyway. He started as an account executive for a firm, making cold calls and soliciting potential clients. In 1972 he switched firms, to one owned by a potato and onion distributor, which lent him the money to buy a membership and trade.

The room had been a fine home for a few hundred members trading eggs and onions. But all the new additions were making it crowded. So six months after the new exchange got up and running, the Merc and its spin off moved. They left their digs on Franklin Street, the exchange's home since 1928, where film star and comic Will Rogers had opened the floor by entertaining the traders with egg and cold storage jokes. When they left, a group of bond traders moved in behind them. The new residents put a biblical slogan on the marble wall by the entrance to the floor: NOT SLOTHFUL IN BUSINESS: FERVENT IN SPIRIT: SERVING THE LORD. . . . ROMANS 12:11. No doubt they needed to cleanse the room of the many sins committed there.

On Thanksgiving weekend in 1972, the Merc's staff members, traders, runners, desk men, and coatroom women moved a few blocks southwest to 444 West Jackson. It was a squat, modern building just over the south branch of the river, a few hops closer to the still bigger, more respectable Board of Trade. The egg, meat, and money traders' new home was a dark green, glass building, designed by trendsetting architects at Skidmore Owings and Merrill, with diagonal trusses on the sides, built over the rail tracks entering Union Station and a bar there that got an influx of business. Train conductors looking for something to do between the morning and afternoon rushes found jobs on the floor in the shadow of the world's tallest building: The 110-story Sears Tower was being built two blocks away.

The trading floor, larger than the old room, was a big, three-story electronic box. New electronic price boards displayed the prices in the market in brightly colored, glowing dots, illuminated by halogen lamps. Runners ferrying trading cards to brokers flicked blank cards in the lamps and tried for fun to start small fires. The south wall had chalkboards, although they stopped taking Polaroid pictures to record the trading. They had done that for a time but quit doing that after an exchange employee was caught selling the expensive film as a side venture (or, in another version of the story, selling Polaroid pictures of half-naked women). The chalkboards were used for the smaller markets like the currencies. They were also there as a backup because computers sometimes sputtered out.

Instead of cigarette-burned parquet floors, the traders walked on black rubber. They couldn't smoke in the pits anymore. That was banned after a controversial referendum. Thanks to the vote, smokers had to leave and practically, almost insultingly, stand against the wall under an overhang. The ceiling, three stories up, was designed to absorb the sound of yelling. In the cloak room, traders hung their colored trading jackets each afternoon on a motor-driven coatrack.

Alongside the pits were the desks. Above those were signs on poles, with the names of the clearing firms. They were like street signs for runners looking for the quickest path to and from the pits. And they were a constant reminder of who was backing and tracking the traders. There was a sign for Barry Lind's Lind-Waldock, which would make a name for itself charging customers discounted commissions. There was also a sign for RB&H, one of the biggest names in the cattle pit. There was a sign for Heinold. Happy Harold Heinold merged his hog and commodity firms that year, 1972, into DeKalb, a big seed company, but he still ran them. There was a sign for Tom Dittmer's Refco, which was big in the cattle pit and also was opening commodity offices across the country. And there were signs for the so-called wire houses like Merrill Lynch.

The firms jostled for position, wanting clear paths for runners and sight lines straight to brokers so that, like pitchers and catchers, they could use hand signals to communicate. The closer they were to the pits, the better information they could get about who was buying or selling and what the big traders were doing.

Moreover, everyone competed for the available technology. Every desk needed telephones. The currency traders in particular needed a lot of phones. Lenny Feldman needed several phones with direct connections to banks to buy and sell currencies. And every man at a desk and in a pit wanted to be able to see certain prices on the electronic boards. Space was at a premium.

The new floor had a first-aid room equipped with everything a nonparamedic could need to keep an anxious, hyper trader alive. That seemed important as the trading got bigger and more intense, louder, and brighter. In addition to heart attacks, they now had to worry about seizures and panic attacks and drugs. Runners on the floor would create another market by buying drugs from people on the trains that ran underneath the building, then distributing them to people making thousands of dollars in a few hours on the floor. It was a rare thing to find people who had both time on their hands and money. It was getting hard to find a good runner who didn't come to work high.

The first day in the new room, traders and runners and exchange staffers took their places. They counted down the seconds to the open on huge digital clocks hung at each end of the floor. The chairman of the Merc was Michael Weinberg Jr., whose father was around seventy and had stopped trading in the pits because he was tired of younger traders knocking his glasses off and stepping on him. Melamed, chairman of the monetary market, still felt he ran the show. He rang a small replica of the Liberty Bell to open the floor. He rang it five seconds too early.

Almost immediately, members realized that the floor needed to be bigger. Now that they had broken out of agriculture and into the world of finance, they could open all kinds of new pits. They would make the floor one-third larger by building an extension that hung out over the sidewalk, with people walking underneath.

Options   +0.08

In 1972 the Merc members moved into a new, frantic, modern trading floor and immediately outgrew it. That same year some clubby Board of Trade members were reluctantly preparing to part with a room adjoining the south end of their trading floor. It was a good hangout room, where any man in his twenties to his eighties could go to sit, eat a sandwich, and smoke a cigar. In case he still wanted to know what was going on in the market, the room had chalkboards with the latest prices. But in April 1973, the grain traders lost their smoking room. They could blame, among others, Eddie O'Connor.

When O'Connor arrived in 1953, he didn't have much interest in exchange politics, nor did he have the time to participate. He traded in the morning and when the closing bell rang left for his job as an insurance adjuster. Many other Board of Trade members left for their second jobs as well, some as policemen or doctors or ballpark vendors.

If an O'Connor was going to go into politics, it might seem to be Eddie's brother Billy. He was sociable and popular, already known for snowmobiling down the Edens Expressway during the blizzard of 1967 to have a drink on Rush Street. After he set up a ramp in the street so he could perform snowmobile jumps, the police confiscated his ride. Many of his modes of transportation over the years were trashed. Unlike his brother, Eddie was serious and formal, and he had better things to do with his time than sit around on a committee and not get paid for it.

But it was difficult for a successful trader to shirk that duty. A Chicago resident knows that if you want potholes filled, you have to get to know your local alderman. At the Board of Trade, O'Connor had to look out for his own interests. The way to do that was to get to know the politicians—and even better, to be one. It often started by joining the lowly pit committee, where arguments in the pit were resolved. That led to higher committees, like the ones that handled membership, the building, the club's coffers, and rule-breakers.

O'Connor fell in with a group of members around his age, in their thirties and forties. They included a charismatic although rumpled and sometimes manic wheat trader named Bill Mallers, whose wide mouth could contort into every facial expression under the sun. There was Patrick Hennessy, a stout man who spent most of his time in an office running a brokerage firm. There was Henry Shatkin, who was turning into the Board of Trade's version of one of Mayor Richard Daley's precinct captains. He had a way of letting his customers know who he supported, and often at the ballot box they shared his views.

At the Merc, a group of men of the same age had taken over the exchange with revolutionary fervor. At the Board, the younger group showed a little more respect for their elders. They did advocate change, however. O'Connor became known as the guy who wanted to hang electronic quote boards on the walls and doomed the board markers who tracked the market with chalk. When the electronic boards broke down, as they did sometimes, they became known as "O'Connor's Folly." But still, he had been one to push the members to something new and, when it worked, better. He spent much of the 1960s on the board of directors, the group of twenty or so men who had more sway at the exchange than anyone else.

Every month the Board's directors sat around a long table to discuss exchange business. These meetings were very different from the equivalent board meetings at the Merc, where Melamed was coming into power, grabbing hold of the exchange as something of a benevolent dictator with a grip that would last decades. At the Board, there were groups of traders with long histories and different agendas, and they met around the table to arm-wrestle for control. The boardroom was usually divided into two factions. On the one hand were the people pushing the interests of "the commercials," the big firms like Cargill, Central Soya, General Mills, and Pillsbury. They sent in large orders, which meant money for brokers. On the other hand were people trading for themselves. They benefited from the big orders, but less directly. That faction included O'Connor.

As they all knew, the grain market moved in cycles. In 1961 the grain trader Charles Carey, son of Peter and brother of Bernie, got so bored and broke trading that he took a job delivering mail after the market closed. Then there was a freeze in Italy, which hurt the production of olive oil. Overnight, the demand for soybean oil sky-rocketed. By the end of the month Carey had quit his mail job and bought a new car.

In the late 1960s, the grain markets were again painfully slow. Government supports created price floors, and surpluses kept prices from being too high. At the Board, the trading floor felt some days like a ghost town, with wind whistling between the pits. In the pits, brokers slowly doled out the orders that came in, handing them around like food to the hungry. Some traders went to offices in the building and took naps until their turn came to trade. Others spent months trying to organize a squeeze, then celebrated when they pulled it off and made a measly few hundred bucks. Slow markets were deadly for traders, especially new traders who didn't know better than to sit on their hands.

Some swallowed their pride and went to check out the Merc. It was considered the lesser exchange and the members didn't often mingle. But the Merc's trading floor was busy, and tempting. Billy O'Connor spent some time there trading cattle.

At the Board, the directors were under pressure to innovate. Eddie O'Connor and the Board's other directors discussed creating some new markets. They hired Henry Hall Wilson, who had been an aide to President John F. Kennedy, and he hired a skinny writer named Joseph Sullivan, who set about exploring futures on plywood, steel, and fish meal.

The directors zeroed in on something very different—securities. It happened that the commodity exchange also had a securities license, and it was gathering dust as the stock market soared. One broker in the commercial camp pushed the idea of trading futures on the Dow Jones industrial average. It was the same idea that the truck driver Murray Borowitz would suggest around that time at his produce exchange in New York.

The directors wanted to talk to an attorney about the idea. They employed outside counsel, Philip Johnson, but this was outside of his expertise. His partner had a brother-in-law, however, who worked across the street at the Continental Bank building and who had worked at the Securities and Exchange Commission (SEC). Milton Cohen was one of the top securities lawyers in the country. So O'Connor and Sullivan went to see Cohen, and he said to drop the idea. It crossed the line into gambling. They came back and told the directors a futures contract on stocks would not work.

O'Connor did some research on his own. In particular, he read an article in *Institutional Investor* and came up with a different suggestion—to trade options on stocks. Options, usually called puts and calls, were familiar. Traders at the Board used to buy options on their futures contracts until that trade had been banned because a group of men in the 1930s had used options to manipulate the wheat market. According to the story, the group included President Roosevelt's dentist. At least, that was the story the traders told.

The more O'Connor learned about puts and calls on stocks, the more he liked the idea of trading them. They reminded him of the old forward contracts that had been standardized and turned into futures. Options also involved an underlying asset—in this case stocks—and were individually crafted, seemingly waiting to be standardized. In late 1968, O'Connor suggested to the board of directors that they set up a pit on the floor for these options. Mallers was about to be named chairman, and O'Connor vice chairman. Mallers told O'Connor to go see if he could make it happen.

The year 1969 felt like the start of something new. That summer the exchange accepted its first female member. Her name was Carol Ovitz. She had grown up in a small Illinois town called Sycamore, gone to Smith College, majored in psychology, and moved to Europe for a year after college. During school, she had a summer job in Chicago at a brokerage firm, the one where her father, a doctor, had an account. He also owned some farms that grew corn and soybeans. She worked in an office in the Continental Bank building, across the street from the Board of Trade. She went back and got a job there.

The New York Stock Exchange had allowed its first female member in 1967. Still, the Board of Trade was a holdout, a pale, male bastion during trading hours, culturally stuck in the 1950s, paying little attention to civil rights or women's lib. Some traders bristled at the idea of allowing women to trade, and one shook a finger in Ovitz's face as he said it would never happen. But Ovitz asked her boss, one of the exchange's directors, if the board would consider changing the rule that said only men were eligible for membership. The vote came back 459 to 183. Ovitz, at age twenty-six, became the first female member of the Chicago Board of Trade.

Mallers, ever the politician, saw an opportunity to use her as a publicity prop to promote a new market in iced broilers. Ovitz had never been on the trading floor, much less traded, but he pushed her into the iced broiler pit. He and Patrick Hennessy, Mallers's pal on the board of directors, told her they would trade with her and make sure she didn't lose money. While the market was open, a newspaper reporter called in for the occasion made note of her "girlish chatter and a regular amount of flirtation." "I think the traders are a pretty open-minded bunch," she told the reporter. "They're looking for ideas." When the market closed, she returned to her office. She continued working from offices for the next several years. Iced broilers ended up failing owing to a chicken cartel of sorts. The price of chicken, many traders said, was essentially set by Kentucky Fried Chicken.

Ovitz was right when she said the traders were looking for ideas. Around that time the exchange introduced a market for plywood and another for silver, which also traded in New York. And they were still also exploring the business of options, which took them to the tip of Manhattan Island, home to Wall Street.

Around Wall Street, buildings housed the member firms of the New York Stock Exchange, whose employees were primarily in the business of trading and handling orders for stock. If a doctor in Peoria wanted to buy five hundred shares of Chrysler, he called his broker, who worked at a firm like Merrill Lynch. The broker arranged for the doctor to buy the five hundred shares. But when asked, firms also did a business in puts and calls. Perhaps the doctor wasn't sure if he wanted to buy those five hundred shares quite yet and wanted the option to buy them. Then his broker phoned a colleague who dealt in puts and calls, or over-the-counter options.

That trade was like a side alley of Wall Street—obscure and a little shady. Firms like Merrill Lynch didn't deal in puts and calls themselves. Instead, the hypothetical broker's colleague would call one of a dozen or so put and call dealers. They were small, sometimes just three people to an office, and staffed mostly with young men in their twenties and thirties who competed with each other for business.

The Merrill Lynch broker would call a put and call dealer like Paul Stevens, a twenty-something man from Long Island who worked at the biggest dealer in the area. The broker would ask Stevens how much he thought it would cost to buy five calls—the option to buy five hundred shares of Chrysler. Stevens would give him a price, say $350, the broker would give him the order, and

Stevens would write $350 on a chalkboard affixed to the wall. Then he'd call brokers he knew at other Wall Street firms, who would in turn call their customers—doctors and other retail investors around the country—to find someone who wanted to sell the Peoria doctor the option to buy Chrysler stock. Sometimes it took a few days to find someone. On the weekends, the put and call dealers ran small advertisements in the newspaper, like car dealers, letting others know what inventory they had.

Usually another customer turned up, someone willing to sell the doctor the option. Stevens would have his colleague draw up a contract, and he'd send a runner over to the seller's broker to get a signature. After Stevens got the contract back, he'd send it to Merrill Lynch. Then he would head to a bar in the area, often Michael One or Forty-Five Below, where he hung out with other put and call dealers and compared war stories. If he was lucky and had had a particularly busy day, his office would have found buyers or sellers for three hundred options contracts. More often, it was fewer.

One day Bill Mallers, chairman of Chicago's biggest and most respectable exchange, went to a brokerage firm in New York to tell an executive there of his exchange's plans. The executive told him that he was sure it would fail and that Mallers did not understand the options business. Every option was different, and finding a person to take the opposite side of the trade took time. The executive found the whole idea so amusing that he called in his secretary, and they both chuckled. Mallers went back to Chicago, feeling certain that, if nothing else, Wall Street's brokers wouldn't bother pressuring regulators to shut them down.

Sullivan went to Washington, D.C., to meet with Irving Pollack, a lawyer at the Securities and Exchange Commission who was in charge of market regulation. That meeting went worse. Pollack was concerned. Setting aside his impression of Chicago's commodity traders as a wild bunch, he had concerns about the product. When traded by put and call dealers, the options business was small, limited to people who sought it out. The Chicago traders planned to involve more people, including retail investors who might start trading without understanding the risks involved. Pollack saw his job as looking out for the little guys, and he imagined them putting down some money, believing it was an investment, and gambling it away. As Sullivan later recounted, Pollack told Sullivan that options as he envisioned them were the financial equivalent of thalidomide, the sedative that was pulled from the market when it was discovered that it caused birth defects. Sullivan got the feeling the SEC was unlikely to approve options trade in Chicago.

But Sullivan and O'Connor pursued it anyway. Richard Nixon had just been elected president, and he seemed to have free-market tendencies in his political appointments. So they forged ahead, with the help of Milton Cohen. He was wary of working with the futures traders, but the family connection helped persuade him. That, and a report put out by some consultants hired by the Board of Trade. They argued that options had real use.

With Cohen as a guide, O'Connor and Sullivan explained their idea to the SEC regulators, who were used to dealing with a stock exchange that adhered to certain procedures, like companies issuing stock and producing a big document called a prospectus, which laid out the prospects and risks. Investors, upon buying the stock, put down at least 50 percent of the stock price in margin. Exchanges processed trades internally. Above all, regulators were generally happy when prices went up.

The men in Chicago colored within those lines as they attempted to create an exchange that would fit the mold of a stock exchange but also look like a futures exchange.

During the next few years, Sullivan handled the details of creating an options trade in Chicago. He got little support for it within the Board of Trade, where he was shuffled from office to office. At one point, he designed the exchange from an office in the windowless basement of the Board of Trade building. By 1971 Sullivan had a mountain of paperwork on his desk, and it seemed to grow two feet per year. Many members of the Board of Trade thought it was a bad use of their dues and their own private Vietnam, a war that dragged on interminably. But Sullivan and a few employees hired to help hung on because they were inspired by the challenge. That year Nixon appointed an SEC chairman who called in Cohen and gave the project a green light. On Sullivan's birthday in October 1971, the president of the Board received a letter from Irving Pollack at the SEC. In heavy legalese, he said that they had the green light to launch a market in stock options.

Inside the Board of Trade, however, the members had lost interest in creating new markets because the grain markets were heating up again, in a big way. It started in 1971, and all the grain traders made a beeline back into trading what they loved. Plus the board of directors changed. Mallers, after a bad stretch, retired as chairman and from politics. The new chairman was Owen Nichols, a broker for commercials, which had little interest in stock options. The directors as a group felt that the Board had dumped too much money into the idea of options. If O'Connor and his crew wanted to form the market, they could make it a different exchange, just as Leo Melamed had done with his newfangled currency market over at the Merc. The Board of Trade would guarantee a loan, but the options exchange would have to pay it back. For their troubles, they wanted Board members to have the right to trade on the new exchange.

O'Connor didn't know if the idea would work, and he was nervous about having to foot the bill to find out. But he and especially Sullivan had sunk too much time and energy into the project to give up. In February 1972, O'Connor signed the papers that created a new entity called the Chicago Board Options Exchange.

The project was already in debt, so the first thing it needed was money. To get it, O'Connor flogged memberships for $10,000 apiece. Unfortunately, the private O'Connor wasn't much of a salesman. Fortunately, his friend Patrick Hennessy was more of a bulldog. When Hennessy knew a grain trader had had a good day, he went to the floor or to the bar and convinced that trader to put some of what he'd made toward a membership in the new options exchange. He sold a few that way, although it was a tough sell, considering that Board members already had the right to trade for free. Carol Ovitz, the Board's first female member, was making a move from an office to the trading floor and considered getting a membership. The trader Ralph Peters, one of the most successful at the Board, told her not to bother because it would be a waste of $10,000. That was, after all, half the price she'd paid to join the Board of Trade. And as a Board member, she would have the right to trade options if she wanted to.

Some of the Chicago traders visited the New York Stock Exchange to see how the floor worked. Members brushed them off, but they learned a lot by talking to clerks. O'Connor sold some memberships in New York, including two to members of the American Stock Exchange, the second-fiddle stock exchange in New York a few blocks from Wall Street. Robert Rubin, a partner at Goldman Sachs who had used puts and calls, offered advice on how to differentiate options trading from gambling and how to justify it as a legitimate business. Goldman bought a membership, and Rubin, a future secretary of the U.S. Treasury, joined the board.

The new exchange needed clearing firms. O'Connor went to the men who backed futures traders, but many were reluctant. They didn't understand options, which seemed more complicated than futures. If they didn't understand them, how would they be able to monitor what traders were doing with them? What's more, with options they would have to deal with a different group of regulators who operated with different rules. It would be a headache and a more expensive business to run. As for New York firms, they weren't interested in getting into this business.

So O'Connor and his brother opened a clearing firm, called First Options, to back options traders. They ran it out of the same office they had used for O'Connor Grain. David Goldberg was a spread trader, one who word had it kept his vocal cords in shape on vacation by swimming underwater and screaming as loud as he could. He also opened a firm. So did Hank Shatkin. And so did a floor broker and trader named Irwin "Corky" Eisen. When he started at the Board of Trade, Eisen, like O'Connor, had been backed by Jim McKerr. When he started his own clearing firm, McKerr lent him the money. When Eisen asked McKerr how he could repay him, McKerr told him to pay it forward to other new traders.

Eisen set up a trading floor in the smoking room, a hybrid of the floors in New York and Chicago. The trading floor in New York was all about auctioneers. Every stock had a person, called a specialist, who stood by a desk and kept track of buyers and sellers and sometimes stepped in to trade for himself. That was different from Chicago, where traders, crammed into pits, competed and fought with each other for trades, jabbing fists and pencils at each other at times. Eisen mashed the two approaches together. Brokers and traders would stand in a U shape at what they called a post. But because options might not trade as actively as futures, there would also be a man standing, kind of like a specialist, by a desk, keeping track of the unfilled orders. At the new options exchange, Eisen insisted, a man could only trade for a customer or himself.

They installed desks down the middle of the room and put posts for sixteen stocks along the walls. The first day of trading was in April 1973. The governor Daniel Walker, who would later be convicted of savings and loan fraud, showed up. So did G. Bradford Cook, a former Chicago lawyer and new head of the Securities and Exchange Commission, who would soon resign in an outgrowth of the growing Watergate scandal. And new members showed up to inaugurate a market that seemed to have little chance of surviving. O'Connor made the first trade; then he and Eisen went to the Board and begged some grain traders to give it a try that day. But the grain room had far more activity.

For years the smoking room—now the Chicago Board Options Exchange trading floor—had been an extension of the futures trading floor. All that separated it from the main room was an open doorway. That was still the case, but it felt different. Only a few people in the pit closest to the door had much of a view into the smoking room, and few people bothered to go inside. For grain traders, walking through the opening was like crossing a border into another country where people spoke a new language and had new customs.

In the grain room, traders could trade for themselves and for customers. In the pits there, many futures traders relied on instinct and emotion. They studied facial expressions and voice tremors to get a feeling for where the market was headed. In the old smoking room, traders had to pick a side—decide whether they were trading for themselves or customers. And a single-options post could have dozens of options trading at different prices all at once. Options traders had to be more rational and study the odds.

Still, a group came around lunchtime when the grain markets were slow. And when those markets closed at 1:30 PM, options were still open, so some traders came in to trade. A few hung out uncomfortably in the posts closest to the door, as if ready to bolt at any point. And a few young traders, with dreams of trading in the grain room, treated options like the farm league. Bernard Carey Jr., son of former chairman Bernard Carey, traded options. He started as the auctioneer of sorts for Polaroid stock.

O'Connor and Goldberg lent $10,000 a pop to traders who wanted to get started. Some came from over-the-counter New York firms that trafficked in stocks that weren't listed on the New York Stock Exchange. O'Connor also lent money to men who had doctorates in math and seemed intrigued by options and the challenge of figuring out the mathematical relationships between them and stocks.

Some of them got hold of a paper put out in 1973 by two economists, Fischer Black and Myron Scholes, a scintillating read entitled "The Pricing of Options and Corporate Liabilities." The title might not have seemed like much, but Black and Scholes had solved a problem that had plagued mathematicians and economics for three and a half centuries. They suggested that prices depend on gory variables like the volatility of the stock in question. It was highly complicated stuff. Traders who wanted to know the price where they should buy or sell an option had to make sense of formulas and equations that looked like alien scribbles.

Soon some traders started walking around with "sheets" pieces of paper filled with numbers that had been calculated using what was to be called the Black-Scholes model. When a broker yelled out a price, a trader in the pit pulled a sheet out of his jacket pocket and looked at it before shouting out a price in return. The trader who could quickly do the calculations in his head, without taking the time to look at the sheet, had an advantage and probably got the trade. To O'Connor, this was still kind of confusing, but he hired the son of a garment district supplier who seemed to have a knack for numbers. The new hire studied the Black-Scholes model and taught it to a few new traders who were interested.

The options traders and grain traders didn't mingle much. In general, futures traders saw the options crowd as stuck-up, while options traders saw futures traders as dopey. When they got together at all, it was often at the bar that had opened downstairs in the lobby, Sign of the Trader. Some Board of Trade members, impressed by the super-strong drinks at another of his bars, had lured the bar owner to the building. Some of the traders from the grain room, where most people favored whiskey, showed up first thing in the morning, before a bartender was on duty. They poured their own drinks and left their tab on a napkin. Some options traders joined them at the bar later in the day. In options, work was busy at the start of the day, then it got slow. During that lull, some went to the bar.

The two kinds of traders were soon even further separated. The market was growing fast and needed more space. O'Connor and the others wanted room to add options on more stocks. They arranged for the new exchange to move to a new trading floor.

They saw the perfect place—the existing trading floor in the grain room. It was the same incredible, seventy-five-foot-high trading room with six-story windows that they had seen in their first days there. It was a temple of trading with a ceiling so high that for years, at Christmastime, circus performers had walked on wires and entertained the children of members. The mural of Ceres kept watch over the traders, who gathered in circles under the faraway chandeliers.

But O'Connor was a rational man and trader who knew that any trader who dwelled on the past could quickly find himself broke. He could not let himself be emotional. And that's why, when O'Connor, like his colleagues, looked at the trading room, he saw wasted space. He saw, like other frontiersmen, open real estate. Specifically, he saw potential space for options traders, and he saw potential income for the Board of Trade members. He saw money, nothing more. So construction workers came in and took down the chandeliers and the mural of Ceres. They brought in huge beams, built a structure, and laid a steel deck on top. And they did all this while traders continued trading. It took six months, but they cut the room in half. They built a new, column-less floor on top of the old one. It became the seventh floor of the building. The options traders moved there.

It was a feat of engineering and a crime against aesthetics, the kind of architectural destruction permitted only in a place that always looks forward, never back. In Sullivan's hometown in Tennessee, preservationists might have protested and stopped it. But not here. This was Chicago.

The year 1974 was slow in most of the stock world, but in Chicago the options business grew busier. Some people trading options felt like they were sitting on a gold mine. Customers stopped calling put and call dealers in New York for options on the sixteen stocks traded in Chicago. They didn't need the dealers to spend several days finding someone to trade with them and to take a generous fee for doing that. They could just call

Chicago, where there were speculators standing by, waiting for their call.

Brokers around Chicago were drumming up yet more speculators. At the Merc, Barry Lind's newspaper ads had inspired others to run ads too. Everyone got creative to attract retail customers to the futures business, particularly in the late 1960s and early 1970s. Maurie Schneider had published a commodities cookbook with an introduction, addressed to the "homemaker," that explained that the recipes involved chicken and cuts of meat meant to keep food costs down. After the homemaker learned to make Wiener Baked Beans and Hamburger Stroganoff, she got to the end of the book and found a pre-addressed postcard to return to get a free booklet about trading commodities. When Barbra Streisand was in a movie in 1974 that mentioned pork bellies, Schneider sent her a brochure. He didn't hear back.

Stockbrokers around the country drummed up speculators too—for options. They saw options as a new product to sell to make themselves some money. However, some did so by promising high or exaggerated returns or by indicating that options trading strategies were more conservative than they were. An option could be used conservatively, but it could also be one of the riskiest trades possible. Like a car or a knife, an option could be a tool or a weapon. Brokers didn't always explain the difference or disclose the risks involved. In 1974 a broker who was in charge of a stock account held by a widow whittled her $400,000 down to half of that, in part by trading options for her. He made $40,000 in commissions for himself.

When the trade took off in Chicago, people in New York got interested. The American Stock Exchange, or Amex for short, prepared to launch its own options exchange, although the men on the floor there didn't seem to understand options like the men in Chicago did. Many saw options as being just like stocks, as something that gained or lost value. Whereas the traders in Chicago saw something else—the link between stock and options prices.

They seemed to always offer better prices than the New York traders did.

The Amex hired a lawyer named William "Bill" Brodsky, who had become interested in options. He traveled to Chicago, visited the trading floor, and was enthralled. In New York, traders polished their pedigrees. The specialists passed down businesses from father to son. But in Chicago many traders had no pedigree. If they were bright, willing, and fearless, Eddie O'Connor and others like him advanced them some money and sent them off to trade.

Brodsky met with Eddie O'Connor and his brother Billy. Besides trading themselves, they guaranteed the trades of grain traders, and now options traders as well. Brodsky asked if the O'Connors would set up an office in New York, to back traders there. O'Connor turned him down. He was making money, but he was also clearing many if not most of the options traders in Chicago. He didn't have the money to set up another office, he said. But besides that, Brodsky got the distinct feeling that O'Connor wasn't all that fond of New Yorkers, especially New Yorkers who were competing against the baby he and his colleagues had worked so hard to create.

There was something else too. O'Connor loved beans. That market had been unbelievably exciting. Demand seemed to always increase. In 1972, when he was setting up the market, grain companies made huge sales of wheat to the Soviet Union and China. The move was christened the "Great Grain Robbery" because federal reserves of grain were left bare. People worried that there wasn't enough wheat to feed Americans. Then came drought, followed by heavy rains and a crop shortage, and prices soared.

In 1973 President Nixon, in the midst of the Watergate scandal, put price limits on certain foodstuffs in an attempt to keep prices down. In the bean meal pit, Gene Cashman saw that customers wanted more beans. He also watched the weather and saw another trend that would drive prices up. An El Niño pattern off of Australia would reduce Peru's fish catch and make it difficult to produce enough fish meal, which was a primary protein in animal feed. The viable substitute: soybean meal. He bought all the grain contracts he could.

As he became convinced of an impending boom, Cashman wanted to be sure he had the money on hand to meet any margin call. So he asked one of his nephews to mortgage his home so he'd have sufficient capital to stay the course. Then the market took off, just like he had predicted. Every day when the market opened, it immediately shot up as far as the exchange allowed, then trading stopped. It was called "limit up." The rumor on the floor was that Cashman made $100 million—a nice haul for a former park policeman.

Not long after the new exchange was up and running, O'Connor went back to the bean pit. O'Connor sometimes drove with his brother to central Illinois farmland to check out the bean crop. At crushing facilities he watched beans being crushed into meal and oil. They examined the beans going in. If the beans were smaller than normal, he knew the yield would be down. If they were larger than normal, the yield would be up. He dealt with options business before the bean pit opened and after it closed. Before long, he would sell the options clearing company to a firm in New York. For him, options trading was a good business that he had pursued for the sake of the Board of Trade.

His dalliance with options was a "delightful paradox," a writer later pointed out in a sociology journal. O'Connor and other Board of Trade members spent years trading with each other eye to eye, drinking with each other, exchanging large sums of money based on verbal agreements, and planning for a day when they could bring their kids into the business. "The result is a moral economy as well as a financial one," the writer observed. Chicago practice, he wrote, contradicted the economic theory preached at the University of Chicago, where professors essentially said individuals were motivated by rational self-interest. In devoting time and energy to the options project, the members acted for the good of the group, not just their own financial benefit.

The new exchange did more than create new opportunities for the grain traders. When he pushed into the world of stocks, O'Connor opened a door into the small, private club he had joined twenty years earlier. Now people in New York, like Brodsky, were looking in, trying to figure out exactly what was going on out there in what they had considered the hinterlands of Chicago.

Mortgages   +0.09

The options experiment opened a rift between the old traders and new traders at the Board of Trade. The grain traders were now sharing hallways, elevators, and bar stools with a slew of new people. Some were fine folks, but others seemed more like New York brats. Some grain traders also felt cheated or jealous. They had paid the bills for years while O'Connor waited for permission to trade, and all they got was the right to trade a product that didn't particularly interest them. But the new traders, who had waltzed in at the last minute, bought memberships that quickly tripled in value and rose further. In all, the experiment was a smashing success for the options traders but a sore spot for the grain traders.

But it also served to energize some grain traders. Les Rosenthal was a wheat broker who was only in his late thirties but had already been at the Board of Trade almost two decades. He started during college as a runner and ended up trading next to Bill Mallers when Mallers was chairman. They became close friends, and between conversations about the Cubs, Rosenthal learned about Board politics. He saw the old club shaking off a few decades of dust, with new products and new faces. So when he joined the board of directors and they discussed what new futures pits they could open, he was enthusiastic when the discussion turned to futures on Treasury bonds. For this they decided to seek professional help—from an economist.

The staff people the Board of Trade had employed over the years often felt like they were valets at a country club carrying the bags for members. It was a tough place to work: In this organization, every member was an owner, so a staff person had 1,402 bosses. E. B. Harris had worked there before he departed for the Mercantile and its mere 500 bosses. Joseph Sullivan worked at the Board before he became obsessed with options and eventually moved to the new exchange. Now, once again, the Board was looking for someone to hire.

They found Richard Sandor, a young economist who seemed to be their polar opposite, oil to the water of the men in the grain club. He grew up in New York and came from a bohemian family. Sandor's father was initially a vaudeville entertainer who sang and told jokes for a living. Sandor was a fancy intellectual who had skipped some grades in elementary school and started teaching when most of his contemporaries were still students. At the ripe age of thirty, he had already spent years speaking to crowds, teaching people about finance, and schmoozing at conferences. He had a doctoral degree and was a young and precocious academic. He started teaching at the University of California at Berkeley, on San Francisco Bay, in 1966 at the age of twenty-four. At Berkeley, Sandor was happily ensconced in a teaching job where his students brought dogs to class when they weren't smoking pot and protesting the Vietnam War. His wife, Ellen, was an officer in the Berkeley chapter of the National Organization for Women.

But Sandor had an interest in futures when few people outside of agricultural colleges had even noticed them. He developed an interest in trading stocks, conveniently when the stock market was going up. At a friend's suggestion, he traded a few futures contracts, then taught a class about them to expand the curriculum and to have an excuse to further his own knowledge. That led to another gig—researching whether San Francisco should set up a futures exchange. As part of that research, he visited Chicago.

The Board's president invited Sandor and his wife to discuss a job offer at the Union League Club, which had a separate entrance for women. Sandor's wife refused to walk through the separate entrance. Sandor didn't like the city's flatness or its weather. He'd gotten his doctorate in Minnesota and had sworn off Midwest winters and tossed out his cold-weather clothes when he left. And yet he liked Chicago's financial district. Amid Chicago's boxy skyscrapers, he felt an energy similar to the energy he felt in Berkeley.

To be sure, Chicago and Berkeley were plenty different. Chicago waqs conservative and traditional. The Board personified it with pipe-puffing floor traders in the same suits and beige coats they had worn for years. The guard manning the door to the trading floor wore a traditional blue uniform, the same he had worn forever. But Sandor sensed change, even in the fashion. Some traders were walking around in red cotton jackets. Some were even wearing jackets with patterns, one with an island print, another with blue birds and cardinals. There were a few women traders. Beneath its stodgy surface, the Board had some youthful and innovative spirit.

In 1972 Sandor took a sabbatical and arranged to spend the year in Chicago, a temporary break from his academic path. He arrived in the midst of secret grain sales, crop shortages, and excitement on the trading floor. It was quickly time for Sandor to head back to Berkeley, but he felt that there was too much going on for him to leave so soon. Then there were embargoes, and gold seemingly rained down on the floor. In the smoking room, the controversial market in stock options was getting started. Sandor was developing some ideas and projects of his own. He asked his bosses at Berkeley for another year off. They granted the request but made it clear that it would have to be his last year away. A year later, in 1974, he quit his teaching job and stayed in Chicago.

Sandor took a road trip around the Midwest and rode a tractor, all in the name of learning more about the business. He wrote a new futures contract for wheat, to be traded alongside the Board's existing wheat contract. It launched in 1974 but didn't catch on.

Many things had to line up just so in order for a contract to work. In the case of wheat, the big grain companies were already trading that kind of wheat at a smaller exchange in Kansas City, Missouri. They didn't want to move their trading to Chicago.

That same year Sandor wrote a futures contract for gold—as did his rivals at other exchanges—to be traded the moment President Richard Nixon lifted a four-decade ban that limited people who liked gold to owning it in the form of gold coins, jewelry, and dental crowns. When he did, individuals could begin to own—and trade—gold bullion.

The traders usually stayed happily inside their agricultural box, gold and silver futures notwithstanding. But one contingent of directors was interested in another futures contract rooted in the world of finance. They were particularly keen on launching a future having to do with interest rates. Sandor bounced an idea off wheat broker Les Rosenthal, who was the head of the Board's committee in charge of finding and launching new products. It was confusing, but Rosenthal listened long enough for Sandor to start to make sense. Sandor proposed a futures contract on home mortgages, which was, politically speaking, a futures contract on a white house with a picket fence—in other words, the American Dream.

Real estate was a pretty boring business at the time. People bought homes and lived in them for decades. Interest rates had risen slowly and predictably. The real estate market was financed primarily by thrifts, also called savings and loans. Bankers there had cushy jobs and often said they were in the 3-6-3 business: They borrowed money at 3 percent, loaned it out at 6 percent, and could be on the golf course by 3:00 in the afternoon. And most kept loans on their books. Thrifts were careful about who they lent money to.

Sandor watched the real estate market change. With John Kennedy in the White House and the stock market booming, people were flocking to California to spend their days in sunny paradise. In the real estate boom that followed, thrifts couldn't keep up and offer all the loans people wanted. Then interest rates went up and disrupted the 3-6-3 business model. When rates rose, the thrifts were stuck borrowing money at 3 percent. Federal law restricted how much they could pay depositors. But when they offered just 3 percent, their depositors saw that they could get more interest elsewhere—for instance, by putting their money in a money market fund or by buying a Treasury bill. So they took their money and left. When that happened, the thrifts had no money to loan out. And when they didn't make loans, the housing boom turned into a bust, and the economy tipped toward recession.

Congress in its infinite wisdom stepped in. It was already in the real estate business. In the 1930s, Congress had created a government-sponsored corporation, nicknamed Fannie Mae, to promote homeownership and get people into homes. The government bought what were called FHA loans—loans made to people who could only afford to put a small amount down. Banks didn't want to make this kind of loan initially. So American politicians, who loved the concept of prosperity—summed up by "a chicken in every pot and a car in every garage"—created Fannie Mae to buy the loans from the banks so that the banks didn't have to hold the loans and worry about them. Thanks to Fannie Mae, millions of Americans bought homes.

Utopia was an enduring political concept. In 1970 Congress created another government corporation, nicknamed Freddie Mac, also to promote homeownership. Freddie Mac bought conventional home loans from thrifts so that the thrifts could make loans, sell them, and use the proceeds to make more loans. If the housing market was a bicycle wheel, then Freddie Mac was the foot pushing on the pedal to make it spin. Freddie Mac required that sellers keep 10 percent of every loan, so that they still had an incentive to make loans prudently.

Soon Freddie Mac held $1 billion worth of mortgage loans. When homeowners paid their mortgages, the checks ended up on the desk of Thomas Bomar, the chief executive of Freddie Mac. He worked in what was called the Railway Labor Building near the Capitol in Washington, D.C. His goal was to take those loans in batches of, say, $100 million, package them up, and sell them to investors as bonds. He sold them through Wall Street's dealers, like the traders at Salomon Brothers.

But while he waited to sell the loans, Bomar knew that Freddie was exposed to interest rate risk, enough to keep him up at night. If interest rates were to go up, the value of the mortgages Freddie owned would decline, and Freddie would lose a lot of money. Bomar wrote an article in which he expressed a wish for a futures contract that he could use, as a farmer did, to hedge away the risk.

Sandor read the article and called Bomar. He said that he, too, had been thinking the very same thing. They met in Bomar's office and talked for several hours, raising their voices to be heard over the workers who were pounding steel outside as they built the city's subway system.

Sandor wanted to create this futures contract, but it was tough. Every mortgage loan was different. They weren't as easy to standardize as corn kernels or pork bellies. But then he found another government corporation, nicknamed Ginnie Mae. It too bought loans—specifically, loans held by people whom the thrifts considered risky borrowers, like single women or low-income families. It made those loans only because Ginnie Mae guaranteed that if they defaulted it would be the government's problem. Ginnie Mae also issued a bond.

Sandor realized something. When interest rates went up, the mortgages lost value. Whether they were loans or bonds, they were worth less. No investor wanted to buy loans paying 6 percent interest when he could pay the same amount and buy loans paying 7 percent. If a thrift or Bomar wanted to sell those loans, they'd have to sell them at a discount. The same was true for the bonds issued by Ginnie Mae. And because the government guaranteed the loans at Ginnie Mae, they were all, for practical purposes, identical. They were standardized, just like corn kernels.

So Sandor used those bonds as a proxy for mortgages. He wrote a futures contract on Ginnie Mae bonds. It was, more importantly, a futures contract whose value rose and fell with interest rates.

He presented this contract to the members of the Board of Trade, explaining that it was a little different from what they were used to. When interest rates went up, he told them, bond prices fell. The reaction: What? How can that be?

Rosenthal didn't get bogged down waiting for explanations. Instead, schooled in the ways of Chicago politics, he stacked the committee that the new contract needed to clear—the financial instruments committee—with his friends. One day the committee members prepared to vote on whether they should devote floor space and resources to this project. One of the committee members was in the washroom when another told him to be in Les's office at 11:00 AM and to vote yes. The first member didn't know what the vote was about, but he showed up and voted yes. When he learned what he had voted for, he doubted it would actually succeed.

From the committee, the Ginnie Mae proposal went to the board of directors. The board was led by Frederick Uhlmann, whose family had been in the grain business for generations. Rosenthal approached the directors like a political pro. He wrote a "Dear Colleague" letter, like the ones that members of Congress write when they want to get a bill passed. He explained why he thought Ginnie Mae futures were a good idea. He ultimately got the directors to approve, but they still had to get the okay from Washington, D.C. There they walked into a political firestorm.

In 1974 politicians were looking for answers to explain high commodity prices, which had inspired housewives to picket outside of the Chicago Mercantile Exchange building on Jackson Street. Mrs. Ethel Rosen, who headed up the group called the Women's War on Prices, urged passersby to write to congressmen and the president, Richard Nixon, to demand cheaper food prices. Women around her held signs and called for a one-week meat boycott. Exchange employees offered the picketers sweet rolls and beef sandwiches, but Rosen and her clan were not amused.

On the surface, it looked like traders in Chicago were to blame for the volatility. Looking for answers, politicians scrutinized this group and deemed it a wild bunch with little oversight. The traders reported to the Commodity Exchange Authority, an often-forgotten division whose offices were buried in the basement of the Department of Agriculture. The twenty bureaucrats there had an ancient buzzer communication system. They rubber-stamped stacks of paper and lived happily in the background of Washington as civil servants collecting paychecks and doing their job with limited resources. They had another office in the Chicago Board of Trade building, also in the basement. In Chicago, they paid rent to the very exchange they regulated.

Suddenly those civil servants were in the public eye. That was around the time someone noticed that futures traders had expanded beyond traditional farm products and into silver and foreign currencies and sugar and cocoa. They were trading in a loophole, operating with no oversight except their own. Congress decided it was high time to scrap the old Commodity Exchange Authority and create a new regulatory agency.

Leo Melamed was quickly in Washington befriending politicians, defending futures traders, and trying to shape the new agency. In May 1974, he testified in front of the Senate Agriculture Committee to fight for self-regulation and against government meddling. Melamed had become a huge fan of Milton Friedman, so much so that he probably would have mowed Friedman's lawn had he asked—or rather, had he paid him enough. Melamed spoke to the senators with his characteristic flourish, erasing memories of the onion scandal with a showy display of patriotism: "Mr. Chairman, there are no commodity exchanges in Moscow; there is no Peking Duck Exchange in China; there is no Havana Cigar Exchange." The public relations department at the Mercantile promptly turned that remark into a marketing campaign and published posters with comical, staged photographs showing what a Peking duck exchange or cigar exchange might look like.

The Board's outside lawyer, Philip Johnson, holed up at the Madison Hotel in Washington, also trying to shape the new regulatory agency. He lobbied to implant two ideas in the law creating the agency. First, he wanted to redefine the word "commodity." Previously, something became a "commodity" when its name was added to a list of what Congress considered commodities, and to date, most of the items on that list had been farm products. But commodities didn't have to be agricultural, he argued. Anything that could be standardized fit the bill. That included securities, like bonds and stocks. Johnson crafted a purposefully vague definition of "commodity." He had futures on securities in mind, but he tried not to mention that because it was a touchy issue. A commodity became any good or article and "all services, rights, and interests." That could be anything—except onions. Futures on onions remained banned.

The second point Johnson emphasized was that futures were futures contracts above all else—and that all of them should be regulated by one agency. On the one hand, this was a bit absurd. Futures contracts on corn, if held long enough, became good for corn. The same was true for pork bellies. That was why they were regulated by the Agriculture Department. And if there were to be futures on securities, that fell into the domain of the Securities and Exchange Commission. But by that logic, Johnson argued, futures contracts would end up having dozens of regulators, which would cause huge headaches and costs. He pointed out that only a fraction of the people in the futures business held contracts in order to take delivery of physical commodities. Most traders got out of the market before they collected anything. Few could even recognize a soybean. They traded futures, not the underlying commodities. There was one insurance commission that oversaw all insurance companies, whatever they protected, whether it was homes, cars, or jewelry. Futures regulation, he argued, should work the same way.

Both points made their way into the law. Johnson wanted to call the new regulatory agency the Futures Trading Commission, but the acronym FTC was already being used in Washington by the Federal Trade Commission. So they called it the Commodity Futures Trading Commission, which, some people later remarked, sounded as if those naming the agency couldn't figure out whether it oversaw commodities or futures.

The new agency was voted into existence in the fall of 1974, shortly after President Nixon resigned, and the bill passed and was signed by new president Gerald Ford. He appointed a chairman, a California lawyer and state assemblyman named William Bagley. Bagley had few staff members, no body of law, and no knowledge of the subject he was to oversee. He looked at the law's definition of commodity and joked that it was broad enough to allow futures on hookers or haircuts. And in fact, one of his first tasks was deciding whether the CFTC should allow futures on Ginnie Maes. He gave the agency's okay to trade them. Lawyers at the Securities and Exchange Commission immediately threatened to sue the new agency over jurisdiction, but Bagley held his ground.

After being approved, the Ginnie Mae futures contract needed traders. People were far more interested in trading gold. Both Chicago exchanges started trading gold the day it was allowed in 1975 to capitalize on the growing gold fever. To come up with people to trade the Ginnie Mae futures contracts, Rosenthal suggested that they create provisional memberships for that pit. The provisional members would have no vote in exchange affairs, and the memberships would expire after six months.

It was tough for members to imagine who might want to trade something so confusing, much less spend $5,000 and six months doing it. But Richard Sandor had a secret weapon: charm. He gave a talk in a small lecture room at Northwestern University in a building just north of the Loop. A few dozen people came. He pulled out his charisma and spun a convincing tale. It's not often that people get second chances in life, he told them. This was one of those rare times. The Board had created the options exchange and sold memberships for $10,000. A year later they were worth $80,000. You didn't take that chance, he said, so take this one.

Rosenthal and Sandor ran a newspaper ad that, playing on the name Ginnie Mae, showed a woman winking seductively and saying there was no longer anything "plain grain" about the Board of Trade. Inside the Board, the ad was read as an insult. But Sandor convinced himself that it represented the future. While writing the contract, he had caught the trading bug. When the market launched, he resigned his position as the Board of Trade's economist and became a member of the Board, acquiring a yellow badge. He spent some time around the corn pit, where the other traders ignored his trading acronym, his initials "RLS," and instead wrote "DOC" on the cards—as in "doctor," the guy on the floor with a doctoral degree. He got a job at Continental Grain heading up a new financial products unit and moved near the Ginnie Mae pit to drum up customers. And he lured nineteen people to the pit, set up in the former smoking room, to start trading in October 1975. Lee Stern's son Jeffrey, a full member, decided to give the pit a try. So did a man named Ray Cahnman.

Cahnman, a tennis player and math major, had the mind of a computer. He was thirty years old, had black hair and a brown beard, and hailed from a middle-class South Side neighborhood where doctors and steel workers lived side by side. He worked three months at a steel mill, packaging steel and sandblasting steel rods. He also packed in business school, the Army, and marriage to a schoolteacher. They bought a home in the far South Side neighborhood of Beverly, where many Board men lived. Cahnman had never thought much about the Board of Trade, and when he did he thought of it as being for farmers. But then he ran into an old tennis friend who traded and who invited him to visit.

Six years after graduating, Cahnman worked for a computer consulting company and had an evening job teaching tennis. The company he worked for had a database with interest rates that was accessible on a computer with a time-sharing terminal—this was, remember, when computers were barely out of the typewriter stage. His boss sent him to make a sales call at the Board of Trade, where he'd heard they were doing something with interest rates. Cahnman tried to speak to Sandor, but instead the receptionist told him he should check out a lecture Sandor was giving. Cahnman went and was hooked. He wanted independence and freedom, not a life of making small talk with a boss. He went home and told his wife he was going to trade.

Cahnman hoped to make $15,000 a year. He told himself that if he ever had $100,000, he would retire and play tennis full-time. But first, he needed a clearing firm to back him. For years, that had been easy to find. Someone would guarantee a young trader because he usually had a close friend or relative around. But the people Cahnman approached said they would back him only if he put down $50,000 with them. Every new trader was a risk. There was no telling what he would do on the trading floor—whether he would handle the risk responsibly or lose more than he had. Cahnman had nowhere near $50,000 to give to anyone. After paying for the provisional membership, he had just $3,000 left, and he needed that to trade.

So he went to Les Rosenthal, who pointed him toward Henry Shatkin. By then Shatkin had been around the building for two decades and had grown popular. The wild gambler had been tamed over the years, and he was now a respectable trader. But he remained a gambler at heart. He guaranteed many traders on the floor, clearing more business than anyone, even a big company like Merrill Lynch. Clearing traders was its own kind of game. When a man came to him and wanted to trade, Shatkin generally watched him on the trading floor to get a sense of what he was like. He knew all the things a trader might do to hide the evidence of losing trades, like keeping trading cards in his pocket. He had done them all himself. Shatkin agreed to back Cahnman and gave him one of the Kelly green jackets worn on the floor by all Shatkin traders.

On the first day, October 19, 1975, Cahnman was too confused to trade. On the second day, he bought a futures contract and quickly sold it. He lost $100. At that rate, he'd be out of money in thirty days. The loss was actually a lucky break. Had he made money instead of lost it, he might have thought trading was easy. He spent the next three days immobile, watching rather than trading. When he traded again, on Friday, he had a problem. He thought he bought a contract. The man he bought from thought the opposite—he thought that Cahnman had sold. They agreed to split the loss.

After he got the basics down, Cahnman began to pick up more. His tennis background helped in the pit. Trading involved hand-eye coordination. He had to make hand signals and keep an eye on others around him. Like a sport, trading took practice. Cahnman didn't get much practice because only a few hundred contracts traded per day, when the corn, wheat, and bean pits traded far more. By the end of five months, Cahnman had lost $1,000. But he was encouraged because the other traders had done worse. They told Rosenthal they wanted to continue trading but wouldn't pay another membership fee. The exchange waived the next round of fees. The traders stayed. Alongside Cahnman were other new traders, most of whom had family connections to people at the Board.

At the Board, traders were in the agriculture business. They spent their days buying and selling grain even if they never actually touched it. The little pit in the smoking room seemed removed from the Board of Trade, as it was linked to a different world, a world of real estate. Back then, if a person wanted to buy or sell a Ginnie Mae, he called a dealer who would quote a price. Cahnman stopped by the Chicago office of the New York bond dealer Lehman Brothers. The office had fancy furniture and a silver coffee service.

Cahnman realized that they were in the same business. And he believed he could create a business that would rival the mortgage-dealing professionals. He could compete. He had no office space to maintain or fancy furniture to buy. On the Rock Island Line train home, he picked up and read discarded newspapers. When his shoes had holes, he stuffed cardboard in them. Instead of buying a filling lunch, he ate freeze-dried soup he got free from a machine in Hank Shatkin's office. But he was willing to offer tighter bid-ask spreads than the Ginnie Mae dealers like Lehman—in other words, he offered better prices.

Cahnman started trading more and more contracts, the one expiring soon and the one expiring after that. He became an aggressive buyer and seller in the pit. When someone was bidding, he bid more. When someone was selling, he sold for less. Brokers started looking to him when they had orders to fill.

At one point Cahnman held the futures contract until it expired to see what would happen. He paid for his proverbial boxcar of Ginnie Maes. He got a receipt that paid him $635 every month, from people dutifully paying their mortgages. He became obsessed with the relationships between the markets. Trading became all that Cahnman could think about. Other traders kept their distance when it seemed that he had forgotten to shower and shave. He often looked like he had slept in his clothes, and the more money he made, the shabbier he looked, although he didn't see it that way. In 1976 he had enough to buy a new Oldsmobile for $7,000. The next day he lost money. He recovered quickly, and months later he made enough back to buy a full membership to the Board of Trade, after borrowing half the $135,000 cost.

But there was little volume in the pit. When few orders came in, it was easy to make a trade and get stuck in one losing money. One Friday afternoon Cahnman reported to Shatkin that he had a position that he thought might be a problem. Shatkin asked him what he thought he might lose on the trade—what the risk was— and Cahnman nervously blurted out that he wasn't sure, but it could be as much as $1 million. Shatkin said they'd talk about it Monday. When Cahnman showed up in a suit on Monday morning, as if dressed for his own funeral, Shatkin had arranged for him to sell his contracts for a large loss that would wipe him out. Cahnman asked for a chance to go to the pit and liquidate the position himself rather than have a broker do it.

This was dangerous. Cahnman could double down. If he could limit his losses to his net worth, he would be saved. If he lost, he would bust out and have a large debit to Shatkin. Shatkin said okay, but he had associates in green jackets follow Cahnman to the pit. Most of the traders in the pit knew that he was in trouble and crowded around. The bell rang. The other traders screamed and spit out low prices. Then a silver trader stepped in, bought the contracts, and stepped out. Cahnman walked out of the pit, chastened and barely solvent. Shatkin ordered him to trade only one contract at a time for a while until he built up more money in his trading account.

The futures market was immature. It bounced along for a while. Then two or so years after the Ginnie Mae pit opened, a representative from the brokerage company E. F. Hutton placed an order to trade $10 million worth of Ginnie Mae futures. When the order was called out, it caused some commotion. Just then, the silver trader who had saved Cahnman walked by. He heard noise, stepped into the pit, heard the order, traded $10 million worth of futures, and walked away. The news of that spread from the grain room to the Mercantile Exchange and into the offices of bond dealers. That was the start of a new group of orders.

In the end, Freddie Mac chief Tom Bomar, sitting on $1 billion worth of bonds, decided that this futures contract didn't help him. The loans that most thrifts made, and that his agency bought, weren't guaranteed like the loans to low-income borrowers. When interest rates went up, his loans lost value at different rates. The futures contract wasn't a good fit.

But the contract lured new people to the exchange, got them to the smoking room, and kept them busy for a few years. They learned how to trade, as well as a bit about the world of finance. And it would all prove useful. The Ginnie Mae was just a steppingstone to the pit that would change the Board.

Bonds   +0.10

It was 1976, and the country was celebrating its bicentennial. In Chicago the newspapers editorialized about how the country had changed from an agricultural place to a modern nation. Chicago had done that too. An economic storm was brewing that would give millions of Americans the cash or credit to buy clothes, shoes, toys, and everything else. The new Sears Tower seemed a monument to hyperactive American consumers.

The Board of Trade seemed old-fashioned. Its building, with grain-motif decorations, was dwarfed by surrounding towers. The traders were still mostly men, and mostly white. But it too was changing. George Seals, an African American defensive tackle for the Chicago Bears, had joined in 1973. He broke the color barrier. His line coach had told him to buy pork bellies because they were going to go through the roof. Seals talked to Henry Shatkin, whom he knew through a charity, and Shatkin told him to buy soybeans instead. Seals took a spot in the pit, where he played another game that involved getting in a man's face. His afro helped him stand out. So did his size, six-foot-three and 285 pounds.

The Board seemed the place to make more money than ever. The run-up in grain prices had made a handful of members wildly rich, able to enjoy profits like few individuals could. Gene Cashman, the onetime park policeman, spent some of his rumored millions on racehorses, expanding a stable he had started years before. He also helped fund the American Freedom Train, a traveling museum of Americana, and had the engine named for his brother George, who had passed away in 1968. Out of his earnings, Lee Stern started a professional soccer team and bought part of the White Sox. When the O'Connor brothers walked into a pit, people waited to see what they would do. They had made millions on their various businesses. Eddie O'Connor spent some of his earnings on a nice piece of land north of the city, and Billy spent some to build a plane, buy a London taxicab—which he painted green to celebrate Ireland—and invest heavily in beer at Butch McGuire's tavern on Rush Street.

The culture was changing, and younger people were coming in. One was Richard Dennis, a young guy from the Southwest Side, a Polish and Irish neighborhood near Midway Airport. He started as a runner at the Merc after high school, then took his trading to the Mid-America; a small exchange once called the Open Board, the Mid-America was like the farm team for the Board of Trade. There, while barely out of high school, he turned a few hundred dollars into a few thousand, and then a few million. By 1976 Dennis was all of twenty-seven years old and a member of the Board of Trade. He wore thick glasses, had thinning hair, and was one of the largest traders at the exchange.

Dennis liked politics, but not Board of Trade politics. He was almost a cliché: kind of a loner, someone who had toted Ayn Rand's quasi-libertarian novels around in high school. While most of the traders would have happily locked up pot-smoking hippies, Dennis believed in legalizing drugs. He also did things that some other traders considered illogical. In his trading, he studied charts to find trends. He represented a new breed, the technical trader. With that approach, he made more money than most of the people on the trading floor. Some traders said he'd be a three-month wonder, like many who had blown in and out, but he kept making money.

He also broke the Board of Trade's code of silence. For decades people had been content to make a good living there and had kept quiet about the wealth available. But word was leaking out that people could get rich. It became the hip thing to be in a bar and say you were from the bean pit. A tavern named John Barleycorn ran a commercial in which a woman fawned over a man who traded at the bean pit, comparing him to a rock star. Dennis admitted his good fortune. He let a reporter from the *New York Times Magazine* follow him around, and the headline would proclaim him "the Prince of the Pit." That ruffled the feathers of some other princes on the floor. A few cursed him out for it, afraid that a few more stories like that and an outraged public would demand that they get $12,000-a-year jobs like everyone else.

It was busy and exciting. Runners fought to get orders to floor brokers in the pits. Floor brokers threw colored trading slips down on the floor, and clerks scrambled to find them and deliver them to clearing firms. It was so loud that traders and brokers, with cigarette burn holes in their jackets, communicated with signals. After every buy or sell, a broker or trader had to write the other party's clearing firm name on the trading card. To let others know what to write on their trading card, a broker who had traded for a customer clearing through Rosenthal's firm pretended to smell a rose pinned to a jacket. Customers clearing through Shatkin pretended to shoot a shotgun, and those clearing through Heinold, now operating at both exchanges, slapped their rears. Prices spun by on electronic boards that the exchange hung on the east and west sides of the room. Digital clocks above the floor counted the seconds. It seemed like a fortune was made and lost with every tick.

Many grain traders were high on life and themselves. Kings of their corner of the universe, they were so important that their weather mattered. When it rained on La Salle Street, the traders saw it. It made them a little moody, and it also made some of them think about how it would affect the crops and whether there would be more corn—and therefore lower prices. The price was affected by weather in Chicago, whether or not it was raining where the crops grew. So rain on La Salle Street affected the price of grains—and of food—all over the world. The grain traders needed more room to work. Their 19,000-square-foot room was feeling small, especially since they had dropped the ceiling to accommodate all the new people trading options upstairs. People were falling out of the soybean pit every day. They were outgrowing their space.

In 1976 the new futures pits for financial products were also growing, even faster. Over at the Merc, Leo Melamed, becoming the Merc's version of Chicago's longtime mayor, Richard J. Daley, who died that year, was making the old egg and butter exchange into something more global. It reabsorbed the International Monetary Market and also launched a pit to trade futures on Treasury bills. The economist Milton Friedman rang the opening bell. More traders started to wear colorful trading jackets. Traders jammed the pockets of these trading jackets with pens and trading cards— it looked like they were carrying their desks around. Their colors became their signature and their identity. Exchange employees wore blue jackets. Runners and clerks wore yellow jackets. Like baseball teams, clearing firms picked their own colors to stand out in the growing crowd. Brokers and traders could wear anything from paisley to an island print as long as their badge was attached.

And at the Board, the financial pits were also growing, despite still being stuck in the old smoking room. Traders there also wore colored jackets, mostly in solid colors. In one part of the room, men crammed into the busy gold and silver pits. In another section, men wearing black badges traded Ginnie Maes. Ray Cahnman was there. Henry Shatkin assigned him a new clerk named Harold Lavender, who every morning checked Cahnman's trades and met with other clerks to resolve any errors from the day before. Lavender had been a lawyer in New Mexico until 1976, when he visited a friend on the trading floor in Chicago and fell in love with it. He quit law, drove his wife, young son, and golf clubs in a red Volkswagen van to Chicago, and joined the Board that October. He clerked in the morning and then, following his friend's advice, traded everything he could. He traded Ginnie Maes in the morning, and silver. He traded plywood, where his friend was a broker, and corn. The grain pits, the heart of the exchange, were his favorite.

In the summer of 1977, the exchange prepared to open another pit in the old smoking room. It was for two new contracts, both financially oriented. The one expected to do best was commercial paper. Practically its own currency on Wall Street, commercial paper was the term for the promissory notes exchanged daily by corporations and banks. The other contract, a futures contract on the thirty-year bond auctioned off by the U.S. Treasury, was considered less likely to succeed. That became known at the Board as the bond market. They were put in one pit, next to the Ginnie Maes.

Again they needed people who would stand in the pit all day and trade, so the exchange offered one hundred restricted memberships for $30,000 apiece, one-sixth of what a full seat cost when the new memberships were proposed. These "financial instrument" members had to be content with one-sixth of a vote in exchange matters. In other words, they would be no threat to the men in the grain room. They could only trade financial futures. They couldn't trade grains or even be in the silver pit, even though it was a few steps away. But they could trade any new nongrain markets that might open in the future, presumably when the full members needed some second-class soldiers they wouldn't mind losing.

People who had Ginnie Mae permits were offered the memberships at a discount. One Ginnie Mae trader who believed in astrology said he wouldn't buy a membership because the stars indicated the new market would fail. Despite that, new traders, most in their early twenties, snapped up the rest. Some were clerks, and half of them had family in the grain room. Howard Sorkin was one. He signed the Board of Trade's membership book with his grandfather and uncle, who were both in the cash grain business, and his older brother, a soybean and soybean oil futures trader, standing nearby. The next day he left his job in insurance and showed up on the trading floor.

The new traders had little to do. When an order came in, a few people stepped into the pit and traded. Then they went back to talking sports and reading newspapers. They played jokes on clerks. Some tied a dollar bill to a piece of string and jerked it away when a clerk tried to pick it up. They tried trading, but it was hard. There weren't many orders, so more than one trader bought a bond contract, watched the market fall, and couldn't easily sell it. The traders often lost $300 and $400 per contract at a time.

The financial room opened early in the morning and stayed open until late afternoon. The exchange hoped grain traders would come in before and after their markets were open, but few did. Ralph Peters, one of the richest traders at the exchange, came to trade sometimes. Hank Shatkin and Les Rosenthal sent a few people over. If those markets worked, it would mean more customers and fees for their clearing firms. But at the Board of Trade most members were happy and comfortable where they were, and they didn't feel pressured to try something new. They stuck with what they perceived to be the more exciting world of grain.

At first, few people who mattered in the business paid much attention to the guys in the bond pit. Most bond traders were in New York, wearing suits to offices on and around Wall Street, and they looked upon floor traders as an odd curiosity in that foreign land of Chicago. That was a place they flew over or through, a town where residents presumably ate corn and steaks and talked about soybeans and sports all day. In fairness, the New Yorkers were kind of correct. That is what many Chicagoans did. Few bond traders recognized their own business in the people jabbing fingers at each other and seeming to gamble with their own money.

But a few did. The investment bank Drexel Burnham Lambert had a broker on the floor, and he did trades for the bond trader Michael Milken, who was at the same time trading a soon-controversial financial product—what would be called junk bonds.

Another group was at Salomon Brothers, the investment bank. Salomon had fancy offices with fancy men in fancy suits. But it also had a trading floor where employees wearing rumpled shirts and holding cigars bought and sold bonds. It was that rare place in the world of finance where someone from the mail room could and did work his way up to be a partner in the firm. In that way, it was a lot like the exchanges in Chicago.

In 1978 Salomon even had a Chicago boy on the desk where customers called in to buy and sell government bonds. He was a junior bond trader named John Meriwether. Irish and from the South Side, he had trader's instincts, which would be made legendary a decade later in Michael Lewis's best-seller *Liar's Poker*, in which Lewis recounts watching him challenge the managing partner to a $10-million hand of Liar's Poker, a bluffing game. "He wore the same blank half-tense expression," Lewis wrote, "when he won as he did when he lost." That was the Chicago trader's poker face, and it seemed like sheer chance that he ended up in New York. But he did, and he was trading government bonds at the same time that Chicago traders were.

Salomon was the biggest bond broker on Wall Street. Its employees traded mortgage bonds as well as government bonds. Salomon's customers were companies putting surplus funds in government bonds or pension funds preserving retirement accounts for police officers, firefighters, and teachers. When a customer called and asked for the price at which they could buy or sell Treasury bonds, the price the Salomon trader gave was probably the best price the caller could hope to find. Salomon traders made the market.

Then the Chicago traders started trading bond futures—essentially the same thing on layaway. A buyer who held on to the futures contract would get bonds, so Salomon had competition. Customers started looking at the price in Chicago and comparing it to the one they got when they called Salomon.

And the Salomon traders, led by Meriwether, saw a way to make some easy money. They set up a desk on the Salomon trading floor, where they bought cheap bond futures and sold Treasury bonds, and vice versa. They did the exact same thing that currency traders in Chicago had done. They "arbed"—they made money on the price differences between the two markets.

By 1979, Chicago's trading floors were bustling. At the Merc, in the cattle pit, prices skyrocketed. Tom Dittmer's Refco had a client, the brand-new first lady of Arkansas, Hillary Clinton. She started an account with a Refco broker in Arkansas and put $1,000 into it. Her trading was outstanding, or winning trades landed somehow in her account. Her broker and Refco would later get in trouble for bad record-keeping, and a member of the *Wall Street Journal*'s editorial board would, when Clinton was campaigning to become senator of New York State, question whether Clinton was well advised and lucky in the futures market or "took a fat bribe." At the Board, in the wheat pit, prices also took off. Regulators sent letters to several traders, one of whom was Les Rosenthal, who was vice chairman of the exchange, because it looked like they had a corner on the wheat market. Regulators temporarily halted trading. The silver pit was loud because the billionaire Hunt brothers were buying metal in huge quantities. And a reporter from *Time* magazine followed Ray Cahnman around as he ran between the Ginnie Mae and bond pits. She watched him, in seconds, make $20,000. The card in his pocket showed he owned futures contracts with a notional value of $100 million.

Yet trading in bonds remained sporadic and erratic. Then came "Tall Paul." That August, Paul Volcker, a six-foot-seven banker, became chairman of the Federal Reserve Board and decided to fight inflation in a big way. On a Saturday that October, he called an unusual weekend press conference and announced some moves intended to slow inflation, in part by raising interest rates. Overnight, the bond business went berserk.

And when bond prices went haywire, the banks that had been trading futures suddenly looked very smart. International Business Machines had just announced plans to borrow $1 billion. Several banks and large dealers on Wall Street had committed to buying IBM's bonds in order to resell them. When interest rates went up, they were stuck with the bonds, and some took huge losses. But a few, including Salomon, where Meriwether's team was trading, were spared because they had hedged using futures. That was the tipping point. Even though bond traders at Wall Street firms worked in separate buildings in Manhattan and could pass each other on the street and never know it, word of the money got around. It became more acceptable to trade futures. In the pit, more orders came in. Traders had less time to read the paper. Banks set up desks on the floor. The bond pit brought Wall Street to Chicago.

Around the time the bond market took off, some people started using a certain word around the building. Richard Sandor, the former Board of Trade economist, believed that he coined the term "derivatives." He said he used it as a mathematician might, to mean a modified equation. Some believed that it was used by bankers who hated futures and options. These bankers, it was said, thought futures referred to eggs and pork bellies, and they wanted a word to connote high finance. However it happened, people started using the word "derivatives" to describe contracts whose value was derived from some underlying thing—a commodity— like eggs or a bond.

The financial markets were different from the food markets: They were many times bigger and involved much more money. The traders in the bond pit—and it was increasingly the bond pit as commercial paper petered out—were on the cusp of something big. They had opportunities to make money that dwarfed those in the grain room, but they also had far greater risk. If the corn pit was a Ford car and the bean pit a Maserati, the bond pit would be a jumbo jet.

The New York Stock Exchange made plans to open a futures exchange and bring the financial futures trade to New York. But they were missing an ingredient—all the Chicago traders. They came to the Loop every morning by train, bus, and car. They filed into the exchange buildings, they competed for orders, they screamed and yelled, and they took risks. When banks sent orders, traders in Chicago filled them. When the banks wanted to sell, the traders bought. When banks wanted to buy, Chicago's traders sold. The new exchange in New York didn't have hundreds of people willing to risk their own money and trade against major institutions. The Chicago Board of Trade did, even though few understood that they had taken on some of the biggest financial interests in the world.

Stocks	+0.11

By 1980 the floor at the Merc was a series of clubs within a club. The meat pits were the old-school club. The hog pit was small, with a dozen men in it. One was Vince Schreiber, a likable broker some called "Vince the Prince." He made friends everywhere. While kicking back at a bar in Wisconsin, he liked the bartender, Terrence "Terry" Duffy, an Irish kid from the South Side. Schreiber brought in Duffy that year to be a runner for $58 a week.

The live cattle and belly pits were bigger, with a few dozen men in each. They had the exchange's older guard, including Bill Henner. Over the years his temper had become sharper. Many traders were intimidated by him, although some of his own clerks learned to appreciate his power in the room and how it rubbed off on them. Every morning clerks representing different traders met to resolve trading errors made the day before. When a mistake involved Henner, clerks approached with fear in their eyes. Meeting Bill Henner became a rite of passage for new clerks. Typically a man at a desk would scribble out an order for feeder cattle, point to Bill Henner, and ask a new clerk to take it to him. Henner would look at the order and scream at the clerk for bringing an order for feeder cattle to someone in the pork belly pit. Without fail, the clerk looked confusedly back at the man at the desk, who was doubled over laughing.

Those pits also had an aggressive group of brokers, among them Jimmy Kaulentis, a decade into his time at the Merc. He was known to some as "Jimmy the Greek," or "the Golden Greek." He had developed a reputation as something of a gangster, although he said he resented the implication and that he simply knew half of Chicago. He knew priests and celebrities, and, yes, he had also worked briefly as a bouncer at a Rush Street bar owned by a mobster named Ken "Joe the Jap" Eto. Kaulentis dressed immaculately and wore monogrammed shirts. He thought the Merc was too good to be true and couldn't believe how much money could be made. So he brought in his brother, his brother-in-law, his cousin, and many friends. He soon sponsored the membership of Pasquale "Patrick" Spilotro, a dentist with twelve kids who happened to be the brother of Anthony Spilotro, reportedly a boss of the Chicago crime world and a model for the Joe Pesci character in the movie *Casino*.

"Harry the Hat" Lowrance was also a broker in the meat pits. After doing well in the belly pit, he bought a large house on Lake Michigan with a glass sauna and whirlpool tub. He ditched his Rolls-Royce, calling it a piece of garbage that couldn't withstand his driving, which included being driven over a median strip. He bought a red, white, and blue 1976 Chevrolet Bicentennial Blazer, and then he ditched driving altogether and bought a burgundy limo and hired a driver. He moved over to the cattle pit and partnered with Kaulentis's brother Dean. In January 1981, a picture of Lowrance with a trading card in his mouth appeared in *Esquire* magazine, showing readers what a boy from Chicago's streets could become at the Merc.

Lowrance hired a young Irish kid originally from Bay Ridge, Brooklyn, named James Place, who went by Jim. Place had moved to Chicago with his mom and his dad, an executive at Merrill Lynch, around age ten. Later he briefly went back to New York, was a runner on the cotton exchange, thought it felt like kindergarten compared to Chicago, and moved back. He idolized Lowrance and got himself a membership, starting in pork bellies.

People in the currency pits formed a different club. They stood in pits lined up along the south wall. Some wore green badges, which marked them as members of the International Monetary Market division. Many of those traders were younger, sons of members working in the meat pits. David Henner's son Bill, the nephew of the other Bill Henner in the belly pit, started trading there. Others there were more academic, banking types from New York. But there were also full members wearing yellow badges. One was Charlie Andrews. After trading from the road for years, he joined the Merc in 1973 and traded from Kansas, promptly lost a small fortune, and moved to Chicago to make it back. He worked in the cattle pit but stepped over to the currency pits after a customer asked him to trade deutschemarks for him. It took ten seconds to hop from one pit to the other.

Next to the currency pits was a big pit for gold futures, which was run by Melamed's old law partner Maury Kravitz, its king. Kravitz, with his raspy voice and now-generous figure, did brisk business there, in large part thanks to a tax loophole that made the gold pit a good place to defer income with spreads and bring down a tax bill. He sometimes attributed his success to superstition. So Kravitz had a routine. He went for coffee at a greasy spoon across the street, a hangout for brokers and postal workers at the big office nearby. Believing it would somehow affect his luck, he never lit his cigarettes with a lighter and didn't park his Mercedes in the garage. Kravitz, too, brought in members. In 1980 he hired Lewis Borsellino, who was the son of Kravitz's secretary and John Anthony Borsellino, better known as "Tony Bors," who a few months earlier had been shot dead and dumped on a deserted road outside of the city. Kravitz hired Lewis as a clerk and then sponsored him for a membership.

In January 1980, the board of directors elected Jack Sandner, from the meat pits, to be chairman. He had started running RB&H after the founders had agreed in 1972 to sell it. They ran it for a few years after that, although cofounder Fred Hertz checked out. In July 1975, Hertz, who many considered disagreeable, was shot dead by his wife at his estate in St. Joseph, Missouri, taking three shots in his Mercedes convertible. After he crashed into a tree, she gave him one for the road, some later said. According to a local newspaper, his wife reported the crime and confessed when police showed up. Right before she was to be tried for murder the next spring, the charge was dismissed after new evidence raised the possibility that she killed Hertz in self-defense.

Sandner, who replaced Laurence "Larry" Rosenberg, a mustachioed cattle trader, as chairman, wore Lucchese cowboy boots with heels that made his slight frame taller. He insisted he wore them because they were gifts from customers in the cattle business. Although he was chairman, Melamed was convinced that he himself remained the true leader of the exchange, regardless of his title. And many agreed.

Amid all the excitement, they were within reach of the holy grail—a futures contract on the stock market. This idea had popped up several times over the decade. The truck driver Murray Borowitz had mentioned it in New York before he pursued futures on currencies. The grain traders at the Board of Trade had talked it over with a lawyer before creating, instead, a new exchange for stock options.

That still seemed like it would be the ultimate pit, the pit to carry futures traders from the world of corn and eggs into the modern world and centers of power. They already traded futures on Treasury bonds and Treasury bills, but stocks went to the heart of Wall Street. It would be the ultimate legacy for whichever person or group could make it happen. For men with egos—and Chicago had many that would be quite a coup.

They never would have guessed who got there first. It made little sense, but a revolution that upended the stock business and Wall Street came from, of all places, Kansas City.

The cattle trader Charlie Andrews had been to Kansas City. In high school, he and his class took a two-hundred-mile train trip to Kansas City, and Andrews visited the city's Board of Trade. In the historic building downtown, he looked down at the trading floor from the visitors' gallery. On half the floor, men carried around pans with grain inside. On the other half, they traded futures, which looked to him like slips of paper. Intrigued, Andrews went back to his family's four-thousand-acre ranch. His father wanted him to be a farmer, but instead he became a cattle trader.

After working for years in a building downtown, the 365 members of the Kansas City Board of Trade moved their sleepy trading floor to a small modern building near the first suburban shopping center in the nation, meant to look European, complete with a replica of the bell tower from the cathedral in Seville, Spain. They prided themselves on trading what's called hard red winter wheat, both in grain form and with futures. The wheat market in Chicago had more people in it and more money coming through. Wheat also traded in Minneapolis. But hard red winter wheat was used in white bread and it was the wheat most often used for export, so the price set in Kansas City was an important benchmark for wheat prices all around the world.

The grain companies had a large presence in Kansas City. All the grain merchants had offices and trading desks at the exchange. Many of the members were brokers or representatives of grain companies. The southern half of the floor was for trading cash grain. Brokers brought in metal pans of grain, samples pulled from railcars, to waist-high tables. On the other half of the floor was an octagonal pit for futures trading. It was like a smaller version of the futures trading pit at the Chicago Board of Trade, complete with a raised catwalk, chalkboards, and a Western Union operator. It was also a more polite version, with fewer traders spitting tobacco into spittoons. They generally disliked being compared to Chicago, much as Chicagoans bristled when New York came up in conversation.

In 1972 the Kansas City Board of Trade hired Walt Vernon, a corporate lawyer who had worked for a national wholesale baking company in Dallas, Texas. The company used wheat flour in its bread, and that's how Vernon was discovered and recruited to Kansas City. He managed the employees for the exchange and enforced the rules of trade. He learned the business and the competitive landscape. In the early 1970s, it was an exciting time in grain markets, with the secret grain sale to Russia and shortages developing.

But the good times couldn't last forever, and the members needed to diversify. It was dangerous for almost any business to rely on a single product. That was particularly true when the traders at the Chicago Board of Trade decided to start trading hard red winter wheat. As it turned out, the Chicago traders didn't capture the Kansas City wheat futures business and went on to other things. But the Kansas City exchange members considered it a wake-up call. Just as Wham-O bounced back from the hula hoop craze with the Slip 'N Slide and the Super Ball, the wheat traders needed to trade something besides wheat.

So the members did what any good exchange members do and formed a committee. The exchange had tried branching out before into other products, like corn and milo, a sorghum mostly used for chicken feed. They needed help this time, so they called in an expert, Dr. Roger Gray.

Gray was an economist at Stanford University, one of the few prominent economists in the commodities world. He was known for having written a colorful and opinionated paper defending speculators after Congress banned onion futures; he compared the ban to medieval European trials. Gray flew to Kansas City and met the committee members over lunch and for other conversations. He suggested that the Kansas City exchange launch a futures contract on the stock market—in particular, on the Dow Jones stock index.

Vernon didn't know that the idea kept popping up. He had been a corporate lawyer in Texas paying no attention to the futures world. He grasped the logic behind the idea. Wheat farmers, millers, bakers, merchants, and exporters traded futures to protect themselves from rising or falling prices. They could hedge their risk by buying or selling futures, often from speculators willing to take on the risk in hopes of making money.

The same principle could apply to the world of stocks. Millions of investors owned stocks and worried about stock prices falling. Meanwhile, pension fund managers, with large sums of money to invest, worried about stock prices rising before they had a chance to buy. They, too, could use futures, and lean on speculators, to hedge their risks.

There was an obvious problem, however. With a wheat futures contract, in theory, the seller promised to deliver wheat, and the buyer promised to take delivery. With a stock index future, that was more difficult. The Dow Jones index was just a calculation. Not only would the seller have to deliver stocks, but he might have to deliver fractions of stocks. And good luck trying to deliver four-fifths of a share of General Electric. Members suggested delivering cash instead of stocks, but that ran afoul of gambling laws.

Regardless, the Kansas City members wrote rules for this new futures contract, using as a basis their rules for trading wheat. Recognizing the folly of trying to deliver partial stocks, they still tried to make the contract look as much like a grain contract as possible. They established quarterly "delivery" dates for when buyers and sellers would settle up. They made trading hours match stock trading in New York City. Vernon hired a local economist to write a paper in favor of the idea and argue that it would be a useful financial tool. Then he sent a proposal off to regulators in Washington at the brand-new Commodity Futures Trading Commission.

Traditionally in the futures world, he would have heard right back. For years the regulators had approved new ideas quickly. But that changed overnight when Congress decided to create a new regulatory agency to oversee the futures business, and Vernon's proposal fell into a legislative and governmental regulatory black hole as the new agency tried to find its footing.

It was just as well, because in the meantime Vernon had a problem. In 1978, as he prepared to finally present a proposal at a Commodity Futures Trading Commission hearing, Vernon received a phone call from an irate lawyer calling on behalf of Dow Jones. Dow Jones prided itself on being a sober, staid company. It didn't want to turn its prized index into a plaything for speculators. Vernon and a committee member went to New York to discuss the issue. They met with executives from Dow Jones, who made it clear they would sue the wheat traders to defend their good name. Vernon also met with an executive at Standard & Poor's. The executive had a large office, and he served coffee as he discussed his company's stock index. It was less famous but perhaps a better benchmark for the market because it tracked five hundred companies rather than just thirty. The Kansas City representatives offered to pay a modest royalty on each trade. The Standard & Poor's executive sent them off to the airport in a limo that had a television inside. But then he, too, sent word that his company's index was off-limits.

So Vernon in 1979 pursued a third choice, to partner with a small, old-fashioned company called Value Line. The company was run by a scholarly but entrepreneurial man named Arnold Bernhard, who had written theater reviews for *Time* and a play called *Bull Market* before he got to Wall Street. He'd worked for the legendary speculator Jesse Livermore and Moody's Investors Service, lost his job during the Depression, and founded his own company, where he was among the first to use metrics to predict future stock prices. By 1979, he published stock data in thick books from a small office in midtown and each week he ranked seventeen hundred stocks and averaged them to create an index. He was happy that the wheat traders had an interest in it and said to go ahead and create futures contracts based on it.

Back in Kansas City, the committee members were disappointed. They had heard of the Dow Jones index, but they knew Value Line and its index were less known. It was complex, calculated weekly, and a distant third choice. Some doubted that anyone would want to trade it, but they authorized funds to develop and market a Value Line stock index futures contract. Then some of them went to New York to talk to stock firms, but most of them went back to wheat trading and left the stock index project to Vernon. He worked on it in Washington, by letter and phone call, between meetings and at home at night. And competitors were at work too. The Chicago Merc in October 1979 announced it had struck a deal with Standard & Poor's to use its name on a stock index futures contract. In New York, the mighty New York Stock Exchange took note of all the financial futures contracts and made plans to get into the futures business.

But they were all held up by fighting in Washington, where regulators were still fighting a turf battle over the hybrid products the futures traders were inventing. From the start, members of the House and Senate Agriculture Committees wanted to keep their oversight over futures. They oversaw the CFTC, whose first chairman, William "Bill" Bagley, a California state assemblyman and lawyer, felt that the law clearly stated that all futures contracts were to be regulated by him and his agency.

There were still people in Washington, mainly on the powerful finance-related congressional committees, who wanted financial futures to be under their umbrella. Their prized jewels were the stock markets, regulated by the forty-five-year-old Securities and Exchange Commission. They saw futures traders as wily farm boys and cowboys who were moving in through the back door of the stock market, where they believed they had God-intended jurisdiction. In this perpetual fight, they tried to draw a line in the sand.

By late 1981, there were two new men in charge of the regulatory agencies. The chair of the CFTC was Phillip Johnson, formerly outside counsel for the Chicago Board of Trade. He spent a year in Puerto Rico writing a legal treatise, then learned that he had been nominated for the top job and was moving to Washington. John S. R. Shad, a wealthy Wall Street executive who was vice chairman of E. F. Hutton, chaired the securities agency. Before that, he started as an analyst at Value Line.

Like their predecessors, these two debated who should oversee all these new securities-related futures markets, including the proposed stock index future. Johnson fought, as he had when the CFTC was first created, to let futures regulators oversee all futures. He'd helped write the definition of "commodity" vaguely for that very reason. Shad was surprisingly conciliatory, although he worried about how futures trading could affect the stock market. He didn't want futures speculators to distort the prices of individual stocks. With respect to the proposed index futures contract, he didn't want traders all buying and selling stocks at once, when the contracts expired.

So they discussed a controversial idea. What if, instead of delivering stock certificates, futures sellers delivered cash instead? To be sure, according to tradition and some state law, all that separated futures trading from gambling was a physical product. When they delivered a physical product, the traders were engaged in legal business with merit. Without anything physical, they were just gamblers. But as Johnson and others saw it, what really separated gambling from futures trading was the existence of risk. Gambling was contrived. With futures, the risk already existed. The important point was that the risk existed, not that the wheat did. Practically speaking, only a small percentage of futures contracts resulted in an actual product delivery anyway.

They hashed out what became known as the Shad-Johnson Accord, the great peace treaty between the stock and futures worlds. Thanks to the accord, Shad and whoever followed him at the Securities and Exchange Commission would continue regulating the stock option market. They also imposed a moratorium on the idea of futures on individual stocks. In return, Johnson and his successors would regulate all futures contracts, even securities-related ones. And they struck a deal in regard to the stock index futures contract: Johnson could bless it into existence, but these sellers could not deliver the underlying stocks, only cash.

Vernon had been waiting for this. With the okay of various members, Vernon's assistant designed a second pit and had it built. They moved some of the wheat brokers' tables to make room. They modernized the exchange's rules and replaced chalkboards with electronic ones.

Eight years after the Kansas City members first pondered a stock index future, Vernon received word that the wheat traders in Kansas City were cleared to trade it. The Federal Reserve Board, led by Paul Volcker, had concerns. A U.S. congressman from New York, Benjamin Rosenthal, called the contract "premature and irresponsible." But on February 24, 1982, the Kansas City mayor rang the opening bell. The pit had some wheat traders and six new traders who had paid $5,000 each for the chance to participate for a year. One had been a hearing officer for the energy department but was now unemployed. A few dozen others joined him, including some stockbrokers from Michigan and stock options traders from Chicago.

The market had some good days after that. For a short time, it was successful. Customers traded it, and the floor in Kansas City was a great place to make money. But to make a futures market work, they needed hedgers and speculators. As customers sent orders in, there weren't enough traders to take the other side at a good price. That was especially true after the stock market hit a downturn. Men on the floor in Kansas City ran out of money. One trader in his twenties froze. As the market fell, he stood still, unable to trade. In the end, they didn't have enough people to handle the orders.

A new group of directors and officers were elected. After that, Vernon was forced out by a group of wheat men who he believed were angry that he'd made them move their desks and pans of grain for his crazy idea. He made his way back into law and watched the idea he pursued continue to grow.

Even if Vernon had been given a few more traders, it's hard to see how the men in Kansas City could have competed. The exchanges in Chicago were close behind. The Chicago Board of Trade prepared for a court battle with Dow Jones to use its name. Meanwhile, on February 16, 1982, they moved into their new 32,000-square-foot home in a glass tower on the parking lot just south of the building. It dwarfed the trading floor in Kansas City. This room did away with tables for bags of grain samples, because increasingly grain was sent straight from a country elevator to a buyer without stopping in Chicago. That made more space for booths, where men on phones took orders from customers calling in from around the world, then flashed orders by hand signals to brokers in the pit. But some relied more, as they always had, on paper orders and runners.

Some soybean traders wore tuxedos that day to celebrate. The governor rang the opening bell with the mayor, Jane Byrne. Immediately, it was a madhouse, pandemonium. The acoustics were meant to improve voice projection but amplified too much. No one could hear anyone else. The men in the grain room had the votes to control decisions at the exchange, but it seemed they could not control sound waves. They would try muffling the sound with tiles and other additions.

It was too late to go back to the old room because the financial traders had moved in. And the financial trade was growing fast. The bond traders took over the old soybean pit. It felt wild, like the old days when meatpackers Benjamin Hutchinson, Philip Armour, and other Chicago barons made giant trades and fought to be called king of the wheat pit. A modern version of Old Hutch himself emerged that year.

Lucien Thomas "Tom" Baldwin III leased a seat. He was twenty-six years old. His dad sold plumbing supplies. Baldwin was a product manager at a meatpacking firm in Ohio before he started trading with $25,000. Before long, he was trading ten times as much as anyone else. He made $1 million in his first year. He eyed a red Porsche. He sold $10 million worth of bond futures in a day and held contracts worth $50 million at a time. If Baldwin was on a hot streak, he sometimes didn't change his pants. He jumped up and down repeatedly and threw his arm forward. People trading from offices or on Wall Street called in to place orders and would start asking what Baldwin was doing.

Meanwhile, the Merc had a deal with Standard & Poor's—the kind of deal that the men from Kansas City hadn't been able to strike. The pit was laid out. Phones were installed. Brokers picked their spots and told clearing firms where to find them. Locals jostled for position. The Merc's stock index got approved on April 20, 1982.

The Merc had an army of traders willing to quote bids and offers. Some came from the gold pit. Congress wised up and closed the tax loophole that Maury Kravitz and the gold traders had enjoyed and in a compromise offered futures traders somewhat favorable tax treatment. But when customers couldn't easily lower their tax bill by trading gold spreads, volume dropped. So some gold traders stepped into the new pit.

The Merc also had clerks on the floor eager to get their start. Memberships had over time become very expensive, but the directors created a new, cheaper level of membership for people who wanted to trade the stock index and related products. When the stock index futures contract was approved by the government, a man named Patrick Joseph "P.J." McCarthy, who'd been a runner, phone clerk, pit clerk, assistant floor manager, and floor manager in the gold pit, went nervously up to Melamed, who was wandering the floor, and reminded him that there were people like him with these memberships in limbo. Melamed immediately called the membership office, where they had an expedited membership approval process. Two hours later McCarthy had a trading jacket and a blue badge that read "PJJ."

A day after the contract was approved, the pit opened for business. There was always some competition among traders to be the first to trade a new market. In the first seconds, a big pork trader named George Segal sold a futures contract to Maury Kravitz. In the next few weeks, others on the floor who were dedicated meat traders also tried the new pit. When the budding New York Futures Exchange launched a stock index market too, Sandner and Melamed handed out buttons at the door that said 15 MINUTES PLEASE to summon the soldiers. They called big traders they knew off the floor, including money managers in New York and Ralph Peters at the Chicago Board of Trade, and asked them to send some orders to the new pit. Peters bought one thousand futures contracts—on the cusp of a huge bull market in the stock market. Melamed, whose skills of persuasion often overshadowed his own trading, was bearish.

Dozens of traders came into the pit. As it got more crowded, some wore cowboy boots with heels to stand taller, or they had cobblers put giant soles on their sneakers—it looked like they were walking around on phone books. A few women braved the pit. The "spoos," shorthand for Standard & Poor's, proved a risky place for traders. The market was more volatile than any other pit on the floor. No limits were imposed on how much it could move in a day. But "danger is no stranger to the S&P ranger," some macho men bragged in the pit.

With the S&P pit, which grew fast, the futures traders broke through the rest of the wall separating them from Wall Street. Now they were in the big leagues. Some of the futures men made more money than executives or even rivals on Wall Street, and they loved that. Again they needed more room and would move to a new building on Wacker Drive.

So few of them paid attention later that year to a landmark event for the Chicago Butter and Egg Board. In September 1982, egg futures stopped trading. The egg business had changed. Small farms had been swallowed by big ones. Growers built confined operations with chicken buildings the size of football fields to supply the supermarket chains that had replaced corner grocers. The price of eggs was stable and predictable, and the space on the trading floor could be put to better use. So one day the egg futures trade disappeared. The era of the egg men was officially over. The new era of the modern speculator was racing forward—on a collision course with the rest of the financial world.

PART III

Under normal circumstances, many people from Chicago had no love for New Yorkers. However, the egg men at the Chicago Merc had some kindred spirits there. Many of the Chicago egg and butter traders talked daily to the egg and butter dealers in New York.

The New York dealers worked in New York's version of Fulton Street in Chicago. A section of small, jumbled streets that intersected at odd angles, northwest of Wall Street, was the food and produce market for the East Coast. Trucks belching exhaust funneled in from around the Eastern Seaboard and unloaded fruits and vegetables and butter. Sometimes they couldn't fit down the narrow streets, which were more the size for small trucks and horse-drawn carts. Eggs went to one block, butter to another. Then they were sent back out again to customers. In the summer, the neighborhood smelled like rotting cheese.

The egg and butter men met daily on Harrison, a small, stone street where you could look over at the Hudson River and see it reflecting the sky. They met in a red-brick building with tall second-story windows and a small towerlike structure on one side. This was the New York Mercantile Exchange.

The dealers there were cut from the same tough, no-nonsense cloth as their Chicago counterparts. Just as in Chicago, they traded eggs for a few minutes each day by putting bids and offers on chalkboards. They traded at the same time Chicago traders did, and called back and forth during that time.

They saw each other too. For years, after the egg season in Chicago wrapped up in January, and the onion season in March, a handful of Chicago traders had gone to New York. Maurie Schneider, Joe Siegel, Bill Henner, and a half-dozen other men would board a plane at O'Hare Airport on Sunday night and fly back home on Friday. In New York, they made their way to the red exchange building. They walked over colored stone floors in the lobby, past a piece of stone where the names of the building's tenants were imprinted, up a staircase to the grand but dingy trading room. Then they were inside looking out of the tall windows, surrounded by a smaller crowd than they were used to: usually just a dozen men, or 150 on a busy day.

Bill Henner stood out, if only because he was an imposing floor broker and taller than everyone else in the room. The New York Merc had its own cast of characters, including Sidney Shear, a dapper man who looked like the old bandleader Xavier Cugat, known for his pencil-thin mustache and for marrying young women. Shear's son Fred worked there too. They also had George Jacobson, who always had a cigar in his mouth. Later, when the exchange fined men for smoking in the ring, Jacobson hired a kid to stand by him and feed dollar bills to the exchange employees who came by to fine him. Vince Kosuga, the man who had helped manipulate onions into oblivion, called in from his home an hour and a half north of the city. Some Chicago members, like Harold Heinold, also had clearing memberships and guaranteed traders in New York.

The New York men gathered in trading areas they called "rings" instead of pits. These were circular areas, without steps, that had a tablelike structure in the middle that the traders could lean on. In addition to eggs, they ran small markets in platinum, palladium, boneless beef, and silver coins. But the big ring, the one that drew the Chicago men, was potatoes.

The New York Merc had a market in the small, round white potatoes grown in Maine, where growers planted potatoes in May and harvested them in September. Then the ring was a battleground until the next May. There was a New England clique, led by a chubby, crude grower from Maine and his heavy-drinking and generous son, who sometimes walked around with thousands of dollars in cash and bailed out traders who went broke. They faced off against a New York clique. Often one tried to drive the market up as the other tried to drive it down. One sneaky trader infiltrated both groups and doubled his profits until others caught on and he got nabbed for trading more than he was allowed to trade by law.

The wild card was that many growers during the winter stuck some potatoes in storage. Although potatoes were easy to grow, they were tricky to store. So in May, potato owners would open a shed, and some would discover that their inventory and potential income had shriveled or turned into a gooey, purple mess. When that happened, on the trading floor on Harrison Street people scrambled to buy potatoes.

The final days of trading were a showdown. Growers came down from Maine. The Chicago men were in. Other traders called. By phone or in person, they all met in the ring, hoping to have bet right about the potato crop. The potato ring was something of a roulette wheel in May, and the buyers and sellers ultimately agreed upon a price.

In the late 1960s and early 1970s, the exchange building's neighborhood was cleared. Most of the food companies moved to a blighted area of the Bronx called Hunts Point, where big trucks could more easily barrel through the streets. Some food merchants were reluctant to leave their buildings, and longtime home, but the city pushed them to leave by saying that any building without a sprinkler system was unfit for the food business. Naturally, few of these indestructible old brick buildings had been built with sprinklers. So the food dealers moved.

But the exchange stayed, and so did the traders. In 1976 they had a particularly challenging year thanks in part to two of the biggest potato growers in the country. One was John Richard

"Jack" Simplot, raised in a small log cabin in Idaho, who made the foundation of his fortune selling dehydrated onions and potatoes to the army during the Second World War and untold tons of frozen french fries to McDonald's. The other was Peter Taggares, a man who had become the potato baron of Washington State. They were growing more potatoes than the farmers in Maine, and they favored the russet, a larger and starchier variety that, for a time, was traded at the Chicago Merc. They traded Maine potatoes seemingly for fun.

That winter leading into 1976 was a wet one in Maine. Potatoes rotted. As some traders anticipated a shortage, they pushed the price of potatoes into the stratosphere. But Simplot and Taggares kept selling potato futures as the market rose. It was curious. When they sold potato futures in New York, they were obligated to close out their trades or deliver potatoes from Maine, where there was clearly a shortage. Their selling thrilled buyers at the Merc because it looked like Simplot and Taggares were going to have to pay the buyers a lot of money.

But the situation worried exchange officials and regulators at the brand-new Commodity Futures Trading Commission (CFTC). It looked to them like a game of chicken that could end badly. On May 4, 1976, a few days before the May contract stopped trading, regulators sent a telegram to Simplot and Taggares warning them that if prices looked "artificial," the agency would consider charging them with price manipulation.

It came down to the last day of trading. On Harrison Street, the floor was electric as the closing bell rang. It seemed that sellers had to deliver 1,900 contracts representing 100 million pounds of potatoes. It was time for Simplot and Taggares to deliver potatoes or buy back their contracts at the very high closing price. Instead, the two growers refused to do either. There was a stalemate in the clearinghouse on Harrison Street. And that led, in May 1976, to the great potato default.

Normally, potato trading was an arcane business that got little notice. But not this time. The default made *Time* and *Newsweek*.

The fact that people were gambling on potatoes made good copy, which was made even better by stories that railroad cars of potatoes were being commandeered as part of the game.

The regulators were furious. They fined Simplot $50,000, but they put the screws on the exchange. They called these officials to Washington and to Maine to explain themselves. The regulators essentially shut down potato trading and said that New York's exchange couldn't launch any new contracts. That left members of the exchange in a pinch. They couldn't trade potatoes, and they couldn't trade anything new. The price of a membership to the New York Mercantile Exchange fell, and dozens of members left.

Some people also had memberships in other exchanges in the neighborhood. Some went to the Commodity Exchange, where they could trade metals like gold and silver. Some went to the New York Cotton Exchange, to trade among some southern gentlemen and visitors who arrived periodically from Memphis wearing seersucker suits and white shoes. A few filed over to the New York Coffee and Sugar Exchange and to the New York Cocoa Exchange, both dominated by older Italian men.

They were quickly reunited. In 1977 all the commodity exchanges moved into the same building, 4 World Trade Center, a smaller, nine-story building in the shadow of the two super-tall towers that had been recently built. They shared a trading floor, each in a quadrant of a 25,000-square-foot room on the eighth floor. They used automated electronic price boards instead of chalkboards. They mingled over cafeteria food like tuna fish sandwiches. The remaining traders of the New York Mercantile Exchange huddled in the southwest corner, seemingly content to ride out the dying potato contract.

Shortly after the move to 4 WTC, a twenty-seven-year-old named Michel (pronounced "Michael") Marks joined the board of directors. He was from New Jersey, the son of a man who owned a frozen food distribution company and had a membership at the

New York Merc and liked to speculate there. Michel went to Princeton. While his contemporaries went to fancy white-shoe law firms, Michel Marks did not. He was sitting around his parents' home, contemplating his future, until his dad got him a job as a clerk for the brokerage firm E. F. Hutton. The younger Marks liked it, became a floor trader, and then started trading for himself.

In the land of the potato men, the college grad was king. An old potato grower from Long Island encouraged him to run for the board, which was a big deal to someone who might still consider running for the board of a high school class a big deal. Marks got elected vice chairman. Two weeks into his term as vice chairman, the chairman had a heart attack. He was alive, but he was out office. Marks was suddenly acting chairman of the New York Merc.

The New York Merc was in bad shape. Marks made it his mission to find something else to trade. After the potato debacle, the regulators limited him to contracts that the exchange already had approval to trade. At home in New Jersey, he pored over the rule book to get ideas. The Merc had purchased the right to trade currencies from the defunct International Commercial Exchange, and he latched on to that. After all, New York was the country's and the world's financial center. Why should that trade be in Chicago? Marks visited dealers on Wall Street to ask them to trade. The exchange set up a ring for currency trading. Suddenly the potato exchange showed some hometown pride. "It's about time New York stopped being embarrassed and mesmerized by the successes of the Chicago exchanges in what are essentially Wall Street's bread and butter and do something about it," the exchange's president, Richard Levine, told the *Globe and Mail*, a Canadian paper. But when the ring opened in October 1978, there were few orders.

Marks had also been pursuing another idea. Being limited to contracts they had approval to trade, he decided to go with heating oil. Several years before, a tall, well-dressed E. F. Hutton broker named Emmett Whitlock, who was usually a broker on the neighboring sugar exchange, wrote a futures contract for gas oil, similar to heating oil. Buyers could take delivery on ships or tankers off the shore of Rotterdam, the big Dutch port that exported oil from Europe. He came to the Merc, ostrich briefcase in hand, and enticed them to trade it. It proved difficult for American dealers to ship that oil over from Europe, and for European dealers to trade in the New York time zone, so the contract languished.

But it was worth trying again. For years the large oil companies known as "the Seven Sisters" controlled the trade of crude oil and everything derived from crude oil. The price was relatively stable. But then Arab state-run companies gained control over the price, which they collectively set as part of the Organization of Petroleum-Exporting Countries, or OPEC. They could limit shipments, and had done so, causing oil prices to skyrocket. A volatile price was a key ingredient for a futures contract.

In 1978 an exchange staffer named Steven Errera, who started as a board boy who wrote prices on chalkboards and rose to become vice president of marketing for the exchange, tried again. He knew nothing about the heating oil business, but he learned. Heating oil started as crude oil that arrived by ship or came out of the ground in West Texas. A lot of that crude oil went into pipes that converged in Cushing, Oklahoma, and from there it traveled to refineries in, say, Houston. Inside the refinery, the oil was cracked, like a coconut. A barrel of oil was cracked into heating oil, the dense bunker oil used in boilers, gasoline, kerosene, and jet fuel. Certain types were seasonal. Gasoline prices rose more in the summer. Heating oil prices rose more in the winter.

The heating oil was fed through a network of pipes into a big pipe called the Colonial Pipeline. Inside that, refined heating oil made a two- to three-week journey and resurfaced in New Jersey. There, next to the turnpike, it went into tanks and storage facilities that were the heating oil equivalents of Chicago's grain elevators. So Errera rewrote the contract, creating two contracts. One called for sellers to deliver the heating oil used to heat homes to New York Harbor. The other called for sellers to deliver industrial fuel oil, used to heat offices and large apartment buildings, to the same place.

The exchange leaders set up a ring and opened it for heating and fuel oil trading on November 14, 1978. A few members stepped in, and they barely traded that day. After that, just a handful of people gave it much attention. One was Emmett Whitlock, still eager to make the idea work. The other was Joel Faber, a thirty-eight-year-old short, ambitious new trader who was the son-in-law of one of the exchange's longtime members. He knew very little about potatoes or the exchange, and the same amount about clothing, although he had worked as a personnel director for the ladies' firm Lane Bryant. He knew nothing about the oil business.

Faber went looking for customers. He pulled out the phone directory and called heating oil companies in New Jersey. The people he called knew nothing about futures and generally didn't want to. They were used to getting oil from the usual source. Faber explained how futures worked, and how distributors could hedge their risk and take delivery in a market backed by an exchange. Heating oil distributors hadn't paid much attention to potatoes, so they weren't scared off by the past default. He followed up with visits and convinced a few men to place some orders for futures contracts. Then he pulled out phone directories for New York and New England and kept calling.

It was a slow slog. But then the heating oil trade got a boost from faraway Iran when young people revolted and exiled the Shah in January 1979 to make Ayatollah Khomeini the leader. When heating oil prices rose as a result, that became a political issue in New Hampshire, where Jimmy Carter was running for reelection and trying to win the primary scheduled for February 1980. His administration put a program in place to keep oil flowing to New Hampshire, and that helped heating oil prices soar.

When Faber called some small heating oil companies, he found that they were more interested in futures and the prospect of locking in lower prices for heating oil. Then trading really picked up. Faber made his first big trade, of five hundred contracts, to applause in the ring. The futures contract became a new tool for heating oil dealers. A onetime potato trader named Richard Saitta, who had spent months in the heating oil ring making no money, joked that he should put a picture of the Ayatollah on his mantle.

It came just in time. Marks was distracted by a second potato crisis. By March 1979, there were once again fifty to seventy-five men trading in the potato ring. But then potatoes arriving from Maine became a problem. The Maine growers who sent them claimed they were good, but buyers in New York said they were bad. When that happened, it threw the market out of whack. Marks and his fellow board members met one night until 4:00 AM and voted to shut down trading. The next morning he walked into the ring and announced the decision. People who had bought and sold futures contracts were outraged. In Washington, D.C., senators from Idaho and Maine introduced a bill to ban potato futures, which would have made them the second commodity, onions being the first, to be banned. Some Wall Street firms washed their hands of the New York Merc.

The Merc was quieter than another corner of the same trading floor, home to gold, silver, and copper traders on the Commodity Exchange, often called the Comex. The Hunt brothers from Texas, heirs of oil tycoon H. L. Hunt, having been slapped down once for trying to corner the soybean market, were buying huge amounts of silver. The price of silver went so high that people across the country dragged silver out of drawers and sold it at shops that melted it down. At the Comex, a trader named Frank Lisi lost a few million dollars one day, but made double that the next and gave everyone high-fives. The price of gold also shot up. The Comex members offered to buy the New York Mercantile to get more room to trade. The directors voted eight to seven to sell, with Marks opposing the deal. With that, the New York Merc almost disappeared, but the metals traders backed out of the deal. And the fledgling heating oil ring stayed alive.

In 1981 they got some more room on the floor thanks to some kangaroos. The New York Merc had a small trade in boneless beef, the polite term for lean hamburger meat. The futures contract on boneless beef called for the delivery of imported beef from Australia and New Zealand. But in August 1981, Australian government inspectors discovered that some exporters were delivering kangaroo meat instead of beef. The exchange suspended trading.

Marks was already at work trying to set up another market. The regulators had loosened up and said they would allow the exchange to launch new contracts, and the idea of trading energy seemed to be working. In October 1981 they started trading gasoline alongside heating oil. It made sense. It was another by-product of crude oil that traveled in the Colonial Pipeline.

But that year the New York Merc hired John Elting Treat, brought in from the White House, where he had been an energy adviser to both Carter and the new guy, Ronald Reagan. He said that if they were trading the components of crude oil, they ought to trade crude oil itself. It helped that President Reagan had just deregulated that market: Anyone could now buy and sell crude oil at any price and amount. The exchange formed a committee that included actual crude oil traders to develop a futures contract. Granted, it was a tricky product to trade. In Chicago in 1964, traders had scratched their heads as they tried to figure out how to write a futures contract for cattle, a commodity that was alive and walking around. Now, in New York, traders scratched their heads some more over how to write a contract for a commodity that wouldn't stop moving. Crude oil flowed into Cushing, Oklahoma, in pipes, and it kept on flowing.

To figure out that puzzle, Marks leaned on Treat, who knew the business of oil, although he found the business of futures trading pretty strange. Soon after arriving, he got into an elevator in the building with a disheveled gold trader who had apparently spent the day trying to start rumors to get the price of gold to go up. "I had to kill the president three times to make a buck today," he said before getting out.

Treat knew oil was tricky to write a futures contract for. And he knew it would be tricky to get people in the oil industry to start using it. If that wasn't enough, the New York traders had to stay ahead of traders in Chicago. The members of the exchanges there had noticed the growing energy trade and also planned to open contracts in oil.

Marks knew the Chicago Board of Trade had hundreds of speculators on the floor. He also had briefly met Leo Melamed of the Chicago Mercantile Exchange, who, before Marks's time, had spent some time in New York trading potatoes. That was before he was transformed, in the futures business, into a one-name rock star, like Cher or Bono. He became simply Leo. His power came from his ability to marshal the traders there to do his bidding and to trade in new pits if he asked. He inspired Marks. To gird for battle over crude oil, Marks held two dinners for his biggest traders and asked them to trade the crude oil future two hours a day for two weeks.

The Chicago Board of Trade launched a crude oil futures contract in March 1983. It distributed cowboy hats to members and made it a Dallas-themed day. At the New York Merc, the ring for crude oil trading opened the same day. It had only twenty or so people in it. Most traders preferred to stick with heating oil because they had gotten used to its players and its rhythm. It was difficult to walk away from a profitable business in one ring and go into an unfamiliar one. However, a few people did it. Charlie Edelstein, whose parents had long been potato brokers—his mother was the first woman broker on any exchange in the country—moved into crude oil. Joel Faber, who had built up a brokerage business, moved a broker there.

The Chicago Board of Trade's contract quickly failed. Members there had tried to get oil companies to change their practices to match the way a futures contract normally worked. The New York Merc's futures contract, on the other hand, mimicked the oil industry's normal practices and provided a better fit. The Merc focused on Cushing, Oklahoma, the oil crossroads where oil flowed in from suppliers and out to buyers. It was already a place for trading, even as the oil flowed. Consequently a small band of former potato traders, who had a young leader in charge by default, found themselves—against the odds—in a position to challenge OPEC ministers when it came to establishing worldwide prices of crude oil.

For the first month, some people at the exchange let drop that enforcement officers would be taking long lunches. The traders interpreted that information to mean that, even though it wasn't allowed, they could go ahead and trade with each other to pump up the volume to get the attention of large companies and the *Wall Street Journal*, which printed commodity prices. To drum up business, some New Yorkers paid visits to Texas. The exchange sent some pretty young women to explain the concept of futures to men at oil companies. Brokers also went to Houston and ably entertained oil executives at the state's great natural wonder, strip clubs. However, others like Steven Errera, who had left the exchange and set up an energy brokerage business, gave seminars about futures markets. He gave many of them, including a three-hour talk at Exxon, where two lawyers and thirty people listened carefully.

Many in the industry, especially people at Exxon, were skeptical. Having traders essentially gambling on the price of oil, as they saw it, seemed like a bad idea to them. But some midsized oil companies signed up. Slowly, people at Sun Oil, then Shell and BP, started to trade. So did T. Boone Pickens, an oil wildcatter who had turned his Mesa Petroleum into one of the world's largest independent oil and natural gas companies. Pickens had owned large grain elevators and cattle feed yards and had traded grain and cattle futures, so he understood the concept.

Back in New York, people who had nothing better to do made their way to the crude oil ring. As trading picked up, all kinds of people came in. Many started as clerks and became brokers and traders if they showed any skill. The ring attracted a football player, a rabbi, a few lawyers, and some business students. Charlie Edelstein liked to hire as clerks street-smart Italian kids from Brooklyn. Maybe some were from families that had ties to organized crime. All that mattered to him was that they were tough and had agile minds.

The more often they offered prices better than those the distributors offered, the more the traders got business. After a few years, it snowballed. In 1985 some senior members of the Saudi royal family came to visit. A few months later, the nations that made up OPEC, the oil producers' cartel, were fighting. The situation had shades of Roy Simmons and his onion clique disintegrating in Chicago's Sherman Hotel. The countries had agreed among themselves to produce a set amount. But some oil countries, regardless of what they had said to the group, kept drilling and selling oil. They kept tankers full of oil sitting at sea off the coast of Texas, just over the horizon, ready for buyers who wanted them. That kept money coming in, which they used to build castles and shiny cities in the sandboxes they called home.

There was so much oil that prices plummeted in 1986. The cartel pulled apart, which led to more volatility. Iraqi soldiers attacked Iranian oil tankers and tried in whatever way they could to cut off Iran's oil exports. The price of oil was as fragile as Middle East peace.

To the traders in New York, this was wonderful. It was as if they had been drilling for oil on the trading floor and suddenly hit a gusher right there in lower Manhattan. Airlines, heating oil companies, and even gas station owners came to the New York Merc to trade. The crude oil ring turned into a madhouse. Traders filled out trading cards as fast as they could and flung them at exchange employees, who wore goggles to protect their eyes from paper cuts. At least one trader took out an insurance policy on his voice. Joel Faber, who in his forties had become an old man by exchange standards, stayed by his desk on the floor and sent his employees into the ring. When he went near, he felt he was risking his life.

From the outside, it looked like the crude oil ring was the most visible point of commodities trading and speculation on earth. And that grated on some people in Chicago, especially at the Chicago Board of Trade. For traders there, crude oil became the futures contract that got away. It was an omen.

Eurodollars   +0.13

In 1987 the Chicago trading floors were colorful seas people. The original networks of egg and grain traders were blending into larger, better capitalized, more competitive groups of people. At the Board, in the bond pit, people squeezed in so tightly that when some soybean traders decided they wanted some space there, they were muscled aside and fights broke out. Tom Baldwin threw a punch over a trade and ended up gouging his opponent with a pencil.

At the Merc, new people filled the floor. Institutional brokerage firms moved sales units to the floor and brought professional staff to work at desks. They understood the mathematics of finance. They handled orders worth billions of dollars for clients.

Others who came were geeky math majors, a group of Mensatype guys with fancy degrees. They came believing they had a mathematical system that would make them wildly rich. Many of these people came and went. There were certain things they could study but were unable to learn. Charlie Andrews, the onetime cattle broker, believed they took themselves too seriously and thought they were smarter than everyone else in the market.

Many came to the Merc because they wanted to get into the business that was minting some of the richest, flashiest men in Chicago. It was the futures version of going to Hollywood to break into movies. To learn it, they had to be on the floor, soak it in, and learn how to run orders from desks to pits and how to talk to traders. The Merc's education department offered classes to the general public, and many who enrolled were clerks and trading floor employees who wanted to trade or advance in the industry. They had to learn the futures basics, like hand signals and rules.

The ones who made it were often the street-smart kids with a sense of odds, the kids who respected and feared the markets like they feared the neighborhood bully. If a new trader was lucky, either he'd quickly lose money or an older trader would throw him up against a wall and bawl him out for making a risky trade. There were many sayings on the floor, aphorisms to learn from. One was, "To be a successful trader, you don't need to be smart, you don't need to be couth or cultured, you need to know how to trade."

Trading could be intoxicating. It was an adrenaline rush to make or lose thousands of dollars a day. Traders woke up at night excited to go to work in the morning. The excitement of the win, of being right, was so intense that people understood what it meant to die happy. The flip side of that was that losing money could be wrenching and painful, and a test of whether a trader had what it took to recover and return. A trader who hoped to survive had to learn to lose or else constantly live in either heaven or hell.

Finance is like biology: Everything is intertwined. No person, however smart, can always predict the future. The traders in Chicago didn't completely understand how the tool they brandished, the futures contract, could interact with other markets. The men in New York understood less. They were a bit like infants about to discover a loaded weapon.

In summer of 1987 the stock market reached record highs. It was felt most directly at the Merc in the stock index pit, where opportunities seemed limitless and brokers and traders were squabbling over spoils. The pit had a bad reputation among some traders on the floor, as the gold pit had before it. Some brokers were taking advantage of rules, filling orders but also making huge trading profits for themselves and their friends in the pit. Local traders who felt shut out got fed up and circulated a petition to make brokers play fair.

But on Friday, October 16, all that mattered was that the market started to dive. On Sunday, markets fell in Asia and Europe.

And when traders filed onto the trading floor Monday morning, they were bracing for a wild day at work. Yet they weren't prepared for how wild it would be.

In New York, investors flooded the stock exchange with sell orders. In Chicago, the stock index pit price opened low, and numbers flew by. Traders were making or losing a lot of money, fast. Many left the floor, cowed, and went to the bar downstairs where one asked the bartender for a bag of heroin. Others stood outside of the pit, under orders not to trade from clearing firms that were too scared to guarantee their trades. Some watched one man in the pit lose his membership and home in two minutes.

In clearing firm offices, people worked furiously to tally up how much traders were making or losing. The exchange's executives huddled and spoke constantly with government officials and their counterparts at the New York Stock Exchange. They included Bill Brodsky, the American Stock Exchange executive who had been intrigued by Chicago traders when the options exchange opened, and who remained so intrigued that he moved to town when the Chicago Merc recruited him in 1982. He became the exchange's president.

In the boardroom, the directors looked at reports from the clearinghouse. The names of clearing firms were blacked out, but the directors saw what the firms owed and wondered which ones would collapse by the end of the day. If firms went down, they wondered if the exchange would survive. And if the exchange went down, they wondered what it would do to the stock market, and the country.

When the bell rang to close trading, the indexes and many traders had been hammered. That night the directors were too busy and anxious to sleep.

Brodsky, Leo Melamed, Jack Sandner, and Barry Lind, among others, spent the night in the clearinghouse's conference room on the sixth floor, monitoring the progress of the clearing system, which was handling more volume than ever before.

The clearinghouse was at the center of the crisis. It was there to keep order, but it was stressed. It usually collected money from losers and distributed money to winners at the end of each day. With the huge amounts of money changing hands, it started early and collected some money earlier in the day. That caused some confusion because some banks weren't sure how much they owed. Some balked at sending over the massive sums requested.

The clearinghouse had a 7:30 AM deadline. If it didn't receive funds by that point, the exchange couldn't open. As the sun came up, it was short money, and Morgan Stanley owed some staggeringly large amount. When exchange officials couldn't convince its bankers to send the money, it was decided that Jack Sandner would phone Morgan Stanley's chairman, at home if necessary. Sandner was in his second three-year stint as chairman of the Merc, but in New York he was the chairman of an afterthought of an exchange whose role in the financial markets was not well understood. The chairman of a different Wall Street firm was said that morning to have asked, "Who is the Chicago Mercantile Exchange, and why do they owe us a billion dollars?"

As the clocked ticked toward 7:30 AM, Sandner called the chairman of Morgan Stanley and carefully explained that the trading business worked a bit differently in Chicago than it did in New York. In Chicago, every trader had to settle his debts every night so that the market could open the next morning. If Morgan Stanley didn't send the money over, he said, the headline in the newspaper the next morning would read that Morgan Stanley had defaulted. The executive said he understood and hung up, and Sandner waited nervously to see if the money would arrive. It was soon on its way. The system worked, but barely.

Already, a dozen people who owed money were in line at the membership office to sell their seats. The price of a seat dropped with every sale, so some offered a few hundred bucks to others to move up in line. There were fewer people than usual in the stock index pit. Traders usually loved volatile markets, but not when they were this volatile. Brokers worried about making errors, as just one could cost as much as a few houses. Clearing firms were nervous too and again pulled people out of the pit.

When the market opened Tuesday morning, brokers sold thousands of contracts, and traders bought them at low levels. The market shot up, making some traders instant millionaires. In minutes, millions of dollars moved from some pockets to others.

But that morning in New York, specialist brokers who were supposed to keep the market orderly were still under pressure. The exchange was open, but trading in dozens of stocks stopped. The chairman of the New York Stock Exchange considered whether to close the exchange. Worried, the Chicago Board Options Exchange halted trading. That left the Chicago Merc leaders worried they would be like the one neighborhood grocery open on Thanksgiving—mobbed, albeit with sellers rather than buyers. Worried, they halted trading in the stock index pit.

But Chicago still had one more open path to the stock market—the Board of Trade. It was still in court with Dow Jones but had a bastardized version of its index called the Major Market Index that was, despite the name, a minor market. And it was open. A trader named Blair Hull, a former member of a blackjack ring at Nevada casinos, who counted cards to increase the odds of winning, saw that other traders and firms were under pressure. He figured the time was right to buy. He went to the trading floor, where the stock index pit was in the onetime smoking room, and bought 150 contracts. Soon the New York Stock Exchange chairman decided to keep his exchange open. So the Merc and the options exchange reopened. When they did, the market rose. Hull had bought at the low and made $3.5 million that day.

At the end of the week, the crisis retreated like a wave from a stormed-on beach. Traders at the Merc regained their footing. Some of the several hundred people who had stood in the pit were gone. Some members owed large amounts of money. Some were still around but were too nervous to trade more than a few contracts. Before the crash, the stock index pit at the Merc had been like a giant game. But the pit became as sober as a more typical office. A decade earlier, men went broke but took up a collection from friends, relatives, and fellow traders on the floor and drummed up the money to return. It got harder to do that. The numbers involved grew. It took more money to climb out of a hole. When a guy didn't show up in the pit, other traders didn't know if he was taking a day off or had gone broke.

Jim Place, the broker who had started in the pork belly pit but had settled into the stock index one, was still there. The year before, he had made $1 million for the first time. He was an Elvis fan and had celebrated by buying a one-and-a-half-acre lot he drove by with his wife, telling her that "Elvis had Graceland, I want Placeland." He turned it into his own retreat, with a 10,000-square-foot house, a tennis court with PLACELAND painted in the middle of it, a swimming pool, and a $150,000 pool house. He bought his wife $100,000 worth of jewelry. He threw her a $50,000 twenty-fifth birthday party at the Hyatt, with a ring costing $50,000 and a fur coat that topped $37,000. A few weeks after the crash, Place held a Halloween party. For $15,000, he had hired an Elvis costume maker to make him the same white jumpsuit, cape, belt, and boots that Elvis had worn in his 1973 "Aloha from Hawaii" concert. When Place was applying makeup to his face the night of the party, he felt that the costume was incomplete, so he sent a clerk to the jewelry store to buy ten gaudy diamond rings. Place's wife dressed as Marilyn Monroe.

But as much as he was living it up, business in the pit slowed. Customers stopped sending as many orders. It grew quiet, giving traders there less to do. Maury Kravitz was one of the many who stopped trading as much. He became obsessed with finding Genghis Khan's tomb in Mongolia.

The stock market crash barely nudged the economy. But it was worse than the crash of 1929 in terms of its percentage loss, and New York and Chicago faced off over who was to blame. Muriel Siebert, the first female member of the New York Stock Exchange, charged that options and futures had turned "a very productive system geared to raising money into a gambling casino." President Reagan assembled a task force to study what happened, and it determined a few months after the crash that stocks, futures, and options were essentially one big market that had failed to act in synch.

Then, as Congress debated and wrung its hands over the role of futures traders, in August 1988 a lawyer who was a partner in a prominent Chicago firm turned the tables on the debate about whether futures contracts were to blame for the crash. A Chicago Board of Trade outside lawyer named Mark Young and an associate co-authored a paper published in the *Georgetown Law Journal*. To the uninitiated, it read like a polite legal paper. On Wall Street it read like an act of war. In the paper, Young argued that Wall Street was in fact running a futures business of its own.

He pointed to products called swaps. Supposedly Salomon Brothers arranged the first such deal in its banking offices in 1981, the year the firm was bought in a wave of consolidation. The first swaps took time to arrange and looked like the kind of deals that investment bankers would put together. Some looked, in a sense, like two homeowners—one with a fixed-rate mortgage, the other with an adjustable rate. Each wanted to pay the other's mortgage. So they swapped payments.

But then someone at Salomon realized that deals like this had potential. They pulled an investment banker named Thomas Jasper out of a cloistered office and set him up on Salomon's trading floor with its loud, swearing, cigar-smoking men. His job was to figure out how to take a heavily negotiated, investment banking–type document and turn it into a tradable contract.

In 1983 Jasper got together with other bankers on Wall Street to standardize the definitions used in these swaps transactions. They formed an association in 1985, the International Swap Dealers Association. In 1987 they had a contract that could be traded. The Salomon traders and others across Wall Street latched on to it. They called businesses they thought would be interested. Some were Japanese banks that paid out fixed rates to bondholders when they wanted to have interest payments that declined with interest rates. Meanwhile, American thrifts lent out money for years at fluctuating rates and wanted to lock in their borrowing costs. The parties could swap. They agreed to pay each other certain amounts in the future. And the dealers collected large fees for arranging the swaps until they started participating in the trades.

To Young, the lawyer in Chicago, these standardized swaps looked a lot like futures contracts. There were swaps contracts for commodities, currencies, and interest rates, just like there were futures contracts for commodities, currencies, and interest rates. The main difference seemed to be size: A swap transaction involved on average $20 million. By that spring, there were $35 billion worth of bond futures contracts open at the Chicago Board of Trade, and there were $1 trillion worth of outstanding swaps transactions. Many swaps were bought and sold by banks in private deals. That, Mark Young said, could be illegal. For that, the bankers could blame turn-of-the-century gambling dens.

A century earlier, the Chicago Board of Trade had been surrounded by "bucket shops"—gambling dens. They were popular with a swath of people, from blacksmiths to newsboys to mothers. When a customer entered a bucket shop, he saw the price of wheat posted. If he thought the price would go up, he put down money to "buy." His money was essentially tossed in a bucket, treated as a bet against the house. If the house lost one bet too many, the operator would close up shop and disappear.

Bucket shops and the futures exchange seemed, to many, interchangeable. One year a man came from Dixon, Illinois, with $35 that he got from selling a cow. He went to a bucket shop and turned his $35 into $1,000. Then he went to the Board and turned his $1,000 into $150,000. By the end of the year, he lost it all. He went empty-handed back to his home in Dixon.

The Chicago Board of Trade members hated the bucket shops, so much that it would seem they struck a deal. In 1922 Congress passed a law that imposed more regulation on the futures industry, but it also wiped out bucket shops because it said all futures contracts had to trade on regulated exchanges. That was to harness speculative impulses to promote hedging and prevent manipulation, Young observed.

What, then, was a futures contract? The Commodity Exchange Act described it as a "contract for the purchase or sale of a commodity for future delivery." And swaps, he seemed to argue, fit the definition of futures contracts. If so, they had to be traded on an exchange. That would greatly crimp the $1-trillion business on Wall Street.

The swaps dealers on Wall Street disagreed with Young's interpretation. They said that a swap was not a futures contract but a banking deal—that they evolved from the world of loans, not the world of trading. They said that swaps, unlike futures, could be individually crafted for customers—and that they could be as different as snowflakes. They said banking regulations were most appropriate.

The New York swaps dealers felt that the Chicago traders were trying to use the law to stamp out competition. Which they were. Leo Melamed had found a hero in the free-market economist Milton Friedman. Jack Sandner ran RB&H, and he had its trading jackets embroidered with the phrase FREE MARKETS FOR FREE MEN. The Chicago Board of Trade put Merton Miller, another famous free-market economist, on its board of directors in 1983. Yet here was a man who represented some of Chicago's free marketeers seemingly promoting more regulation.

They fought it out in Washington, where the Chicago crowd was well established. The exchanges were, of course, political by nature. Politics was an art form in Chicago, with the late Mayor Richard Daley its Van Gogh. Daley's right-hand man Tom Donovan now ran the Board of Trade as its nonmember president. He walked through the corridors of Washington in an expensive suit and surrounded by an entourage of lobbyists, looking almost like a river otter swimming comfortably in a stream.

The Merc, too, had learned to play politics in Washington. When the CFTC was first established, its first chairman, Bill Bagley, visited the Merc and told its members that the way to be heard in Washington was to participate in the process—in other words, give money. They took that advice to heart and promptly started a political action committee to which members made large and regular contributions. They used it to get perhaps one-third of the members of Congress to visit the trading floor, a parade of politicians who came to learn about the futures business firsthand and seal it with a check. Both exchanges hired people from Washington and sent people to Washington. They had influence over their often-overlooked regulatory agency and over the politicians sitting on the agriculture committees that oversaw it.

The Wall Street men had the International Swap Dealers Association, chaired by Mark Brickell of J. P. Morgan. One of the many people he came to know was the economist Wendy Gramm, who was appointed chairman of the CFTC in 1988. Brickell and Gramm were big fans of free-market teachings. Deciding the issue of whether Wall Street was running illegal futures markets fell to the CFTC, chaired by Gramm.

In July 1989, the CFTC issued a policy statement. It tacitly admitted that swaps looked like futures when it said that many swaps possessed "elements of futures or options contracts," but it let the swaps dealers off the hook. It said that swaps were not appropriately regulated as futures.

From that point on, swaps demonstrated what futures markets might have looked like had they not been pounded into shape in frontier times. A man in the futures business traded futures on something he expected to happen in the future. For example, he bought corn that he expected farmers would grow. He traded a standardized commodity, and he traded it in a pit that was a public marketplace where everyone saw his trade. A clearing firm kept a lid on how much he traded. In the clearinghouse, a scorekeeper knew who the biggest traders were, knew how much they might lose on a day-to-day basis, and knew how that could affect the market.

In the swaps market, a person—most often someone at a company—also traded a contract on something he expected to happen in the future. And increasingly that person traded a standardized contract. But the CFTC decided the traders didn't need a public marketplace or a clearing firm or a clearinghouse. Reborn 150 years later, the swaps market avoided the things that Young argued were put in place to prevent manipulation and to direct speculative impulses.

To the exchanges, the CFTC's decision could have been considered a crushing blow dealt by their friends in Washington. But some futures traders got into the swaps business. Charlie Andrews, the onetime cattle trader, started spending less time on the floor and more time traveling to banks around the world, many in Europe, arranging and calculating swaps. Some were, as the swaps dealers argued, individually crafted deals. For example, Hyundai in South Korea had Canadian dollars and needed local currency, won, to build more cars. A rich guy in Korea wanted to safeguard his net worth in a stronger currency than won. Andrews did the math, and the customers' banks arranged a swap.

And the futures traders quickly realized that the swaps statement had a side benefit. More swaps trading meant more futures trading. Increasingly banks participated in the swaps trades. And after a Wall Street dealer at a place like Salomon Brothers engaged in a $50-million swap, he often turned around and made a similarly big trade in Chicago to get rid of the risk. He did that often in a small pit at the Merc that, thanks to Gramm and her commissioners, had started to grow.

The pit at the Merc was called Eurodollars. It opened in December 1981, a few months before the stock index pit opened in 1982. The opening, with the Merc's usual theatrics, was broadcast live by satellite to London. The Eurodollar was a curious contract that tracked what someone could earn in interest if they deposited U.S. dollars in a bank in Europe. At maturity, they got dollars back. For a few years, the pit stayed small.

That pit had one of the most talented brokers at the exchange. His name was Richard "Dicky" Lowrance, Harry the Hat's younger brother. His badge read "DRBY," so many people called him Derby. Derby was a trading machine. He had an amazing memory and mind. He could trade with fifteen people at once and remember exactly what he had traded, and with whom. He made $300,000 a month, or so went the rumor on the floor.

But he lost his business on a stunt. In 1985 he agreed to fake-steal another trader's silver 1981 Mercedes-Benz 380 SL sedan, and the trader collected $43,300 in insurance money. In 1988 two Miami police detectives noticed the car's vehicle identification number had been changed, seized the car, and found the original trader's mobile phone inside. In 1989 Lowrance was charged with the crime. He left the floor. He would try arguing in court that he was so rich that he lacked any motive to steal the car, but that didn't win over jurors.

Jim Place took over Dicky Lowrance's brokerage business in 1989. Place didn't understand wholly what a Eurodollar was or what made the price go up or down. But he didn't need to. He stood in the pit and watched the other traders to figure out who wanted the market to go up and who wanted it to drop. He kept count of trades, and although it remained controversial at the Merc, he bought and sold for himself and for customers. And there were a lot of customers calling in. Business started to grow fast. The Eurodollar pit was an oval divided into two sections. When more people called in, more traders came to the pit and the oval grew. The exchange added more contracts that expired years into the future, and it made more space on the floor for the growing market. All that seemed to limit the market was the number of people who could cram into the pit.

Soon Place was back to making a six-figure income. He lived like a movie star at the height of his fame. He spent $10,000 at dinner and bought Cristal at $250 a bottle. He bought Jimmy Kaulentis a $1,500 bottle of wine bottled in 1945, the year Kaulentis was born. Place lavished money on customers, buying them dinners, making sure every woman at the table had a dozen roses. He in turn received Christmas presents that filled his living room and made Santa superfluous. He bought a house next door for his parents.

Place owed his success to the Eurodollar pit and the giant swaps business lurking in the background, providing the orders. He didn't know or care why the orders were coming in, just that they were. The traders scooped up money like miners scooped out ore.

The murkiness of swaps looked like a problem to the head regulator of the futures business years later. When a CFTC chairwoman named Brooksley Born took office in 1996, she said it looked like banks and companies were making trillions of dollars worth of private bets, and there was virtually no public information about them. The closest window into the swaps market was the Eurodollar futures pit.

As swaps trades sparked losses and lawsuits, Born fought in Washington, against the powerful Federal Reserve chairman Alan Greenspan and Treasury Secretary Robert Rubin, among others, to have better regulation of the swaps markets. The CFTC seemed the most likely regulator because swaps, as the lawyer Mark Young had pointed out before, were arguably futures. But by then the Merc had welcomed Wendy Gramm to its board. The swaps market had grown into many trillions of dollars and dwarfed the world's total gross domestic product. And Eurodollar traders, in the biggest pit in the building, were too busy to care.

Bund   +0.14

In January 1989, federal agents were working undercover in the futures pits in Chicago. One went by the code name Randy Jackson. In the Swiss franc pit at the Merc, by then packed with 150 people, he learned to lose money. For months he stood a few rows away from a thirty-two-year-old broker named Robert Mosky, who had a funny feeling about Jackson. The thirty-five-year-old third-generation trader Bill Henner, the son of David Henner and nephew of the elder Bill Henner, also stood nearby. When Jackson lost money, as he often did, he told Henner it was okay because he had a rich uncle in San Francisco—named Sam, it turned out.

When "Jackson" and the other federal agents felt they had enough to prosecute, in January 1989, they knocked on doors late at night. They sat traders down in living rooms and at kitchen tables and told them they were going to lose everything—their homes, cars, and wives—unless they cooperated. Some did.

The government indicted dozens of traders, alleging that they cheated customers and broke various trading rules. The trials lasted months. Some went to watch, but many stayed away, believing that showing up there was like showing up at a Mafia funeral—a way to attract unwanted attention. Mosky was charged with racketeering, multiple counts of mail and wire fraud, and violating the Commodity Exchange Act. The government estimated that he cost customers at least $13,400 in noncompetitive trades. Two years later, he pled guilty to one count of wire fraud and to cheating a customer out of $12.50 on a trade. He was sentenced to four months in jail. Around the exchanges, many of the traders considered the investigation a witch hunt by overzealous prosecutors. It left people on the floor paranoid that everyone was wearing a wire.

In the wake of the investigation, however, regulators wanted better records and audit trails. They made traders write records of trades on cards in ink, not pencil. At the Board of Trade, many traders already were using new trading cards that made it impossible to erase numbers. There was an even better way to keep records—by using computers. But depending on how they were deployed, computers could change and even kill the 120-year-old practice of trading on the floor.

As it happened, the people in Chicago already had computers on the brain. In 1987, some traders wanted to be able to continue trading after the market closed for the day. The Chicago Board of Trade offered some night sessions and kept the bond pit open late. Jack Sandner said that he suggested the Merc set up after-hours trading on chalkboards and that a longtime member and director named John Geldermann suggested they use a computer system instead of chalkboards.

Leo Melamed was in technology mode. That year, 1987, he published a science fiction book called *The Tenth Planet* whose main character is a humanlike computer. He thought that computer trading made sense. To be sure, trading on a computer would be different. It was quiet, with no farting, burping, swearing, or camaraderie. It was faster. A trader could make a decision and hit a button to trade, without waiting for any runners or brokers. He could trade more than one product at a time and would seem to be on equal footing with everyone, regardless of his height or friendships with other traders. That could make it easier for women to trade, although a few did brave the pits. The computer offered a virtual pit with room for everyone. A trader in the pit could shout only so loud and so far. With a computer, the market could be far bigger, unconstrained by space.

In September 1987, the Merc announced plans to develop an electronic trading system to be turned on when the pits were closed and targeted to traders in Europe and Asia. The next month, Sandner, Melamed, and a few other people from the Merc had dinner at a restaurant in the Sears Tower with executives from the financial services company Reuters to discuss the system, which was initially called PMT, short for Post Market Trade. People started to joke that it was uncomfortably close to Pre-Menstrual Tension, so they gave it a new name, Globex. That night they ended up talking about the stock market crash instead.

But the trading floor had been around a long time. Many people lost money there, of course, and some merely made a living. But some of the people there got rich and were living the high life—making $30,000 or $40,000 or $75,000 or more a month. They spent their money on big houses and boats and Rolls-Royces, furnishings, vacations, clothes, and drugs. If you went to a party at the house of someone in the business, the futures men all wore the same suit bought from the same fancy store. No one thought the money would stop. So when they lost business or the luck ran out and they stopped making as much money and couldn't keep up the lifestyle, it could be traumatic. Jimmy Kaulentis had friends who committed suicide.

Electronic trading threatened this way of life, particularly for brokers. Theoretically traders could learn to trade electronically. But floor brokers, who executed orders for customers, were unlikely to have a place in an all-electronic world. The biggest broker at the Merc was Kaulentis, who had a controversial brokerage business. It started in the 1970s when he and his brother began working together, then branched out to work with some other brokers. They became a one-stop shop. They pooled commissions and expenses, cooperated, and shared customers. They drew investors, including RB&H. Maury Kravitz started a similar group that ended up merging with Kaulentis's, which became the biggest brokerage group on the floor. The groups drew the ire of smaller brokers and local traders who felt that the groups unfairly traded with each other and corrupted the fair and open marketplace.

People on the trading floor, including Kaulentis, were happy with the floor. They weren't convinced electronic trading was better or more efficient than the system they had. Melamed pushed them hard to adopt electronic trading, and they pushed back to preserve their jobs for as long as possible.

In 1989 John Geldermann became chairman, but then Sandner once again took over. He had amassed a power base and customers on the floor. He was also a skilled politician. He expressed support for an electronic trading platform. Then, depending on whom you asked, he advanced it carefully or not at all.

Melamed and Sandner increasingly clashed. Melamed had been a leader and mentor for years. He had loyal followers who treated him with reverence. But Sandner had come into his own. People described them both as smart, arrogant, and politically calculating, and as having giant egos. They publicly denied a dispute with each other, but the tension was hard to hide. Melamed had talked for several years about retiring and finally left the Merc's board in 1991, when Sandner ruled the Merc.

A fight over electronic trading was also shaping up at the Board of Trade. There, the original grain trading room in the creaky, old building was a madhouse. The bond pit probably had a thousand people in it, and they were crammed in together to the point that they couldn't move. Traders arrived at dawn to claim their spots in the pit, and they threw punches over good real estate. It was reaching a breaking point. The bond pit was surrounded by newer pits, including one for ten-year notes issued by the Treasury and several for options on the futures markets. The room was a fire hazard. If a plaque on the wall said it could safely handle fifteen hundred people, there were double that. When they needed to run more wiring, they had to cross their fingers and pray that it would work.

Board of Trade members made plans to spend $130 million to build a new trading floor. But the directors also saw the Merc working on an electronic trading system, so they did the same and formed a small committee to design an electronic trading system they called Aurora. The committee members fought over what it should look like. They decided on something that was almost like a video game, with a screen to represent the pit and icons to represent individuals who were bidding and offering. If a trader wanted to move from one pit to another, he moved an icon. It took a lot of graphics and processing and more bandwidth than was available.

Soon, as often happened at the Board of Trade, there was a new chairman. Unlike at the Merc, the Board's chairman rarely lasted more than two years. In 1990 the chairman at the time, Karsten Mahlmann, won a rare fourth term. Then he resigned days before his company went bankrupt in an embarrassing scandal perpetrated by several executives. Billy O'Connor took over.

O'Connor was Eddie's brother and in many ways his opposite. Eddie was formal and serious. Billy was friendly and everyone's best friend. He wore a badge that said WFO, which some translated as Wild Flying Object. He was known about town for his three decades of crashing motorcycles, planes, snowmobiles, and anything else imaginable. He was a well-known beer drinker with a regular stool at Butch McGuire's saloon on Rush Street. He was also phenomenally successful. Billy and Eddie sold their options clearing firm to a New York specialist firm. Then they created a trading firm that relied heavily on computers, and they sold their stake in that to Swiss Bank. They kept quiet about their net worth. In 1982 the *New York Times* had noticed the O'Connors: The reporter wrote a long article saying, in short, that those O'Connor brothers seemed rich and important and in many businesses, but few in Chicago would say anything about them on the record. And few had since.

Billy O'Connor abandoned the Aurora trading system and struck a deal in 1990 to make Globex a three-way venture. But the Reuters system seemed plagued by delays, so he also pushed another trading system inside the Board of Trade. Directors approved it in June 1991, and O'Connor said that it would be used to trade only off-markets in off-hours and would have no impact on the active pits at the Board.

Brokers on the floor were still suspicious. One skeptic was Harold Lavender, a clerk turned soybean meal and oil trader who became a broker in the bond pit in 1991. He made a good living on the floor, enough to buy a big house north of the city, a block from the lake, surrounded by gates that had once stood at the World's Columbian Exposition in Chicago on 1892. He also made enough to satisfy his budding interest in computers. In the early 1980s, he paid $8,000 to buy a personal computer for his home office, complete with two floppy discs, a primitive monitor, and enough memory to soon run a cell phone. He also paid $4,500 for a 60-pound hard drive.

Despite his geeky side, Lavender believed strongly in the trading floor and in brokers. He watched other traders, listened to the sounds of the trading floor, and took its pulse to trade for customers. A computer couldn't do that.

To be sure, he knew, the floor had problems. As the money involved grew, the markets attracted con men. The day before O'Connor introduced the computer system in 1992, a trader who cleared through Lee Stern's company went on a billion-dollar selling spree in the bond pit, and Stern had to come up with $9 million to cover the losses. And unbeknownst to anyone yet, across the globe in Singapore an English trader working for London's oldest bank, Barings, was on his way to racking up and hiding $1 billion in losses, enough to bankrupt Barings. Lavender, however, was an upstanding broker. He believed that in spite of occasional rogue traders, the trading floor usually worked great.

When O'Connor's term was up, he didn't run again. One of the candidates was Patrick Arbor, a smooth politician who loved the fraternity that had taken him in so many years earlier—twice. Arbor grew up on the West Side with an alcoholic mother and spent four years in a residence for kids. He got to the Board of Trade in 1965, lost money, and left to work in construction. Then he got a loan from Henry Shatkin and came back in time for the wild grain markets of the early 1970s.

Arbor spent the next two decades trading in the grain room and periodically climbing mountains for fun. He liked to say that Chicago grew traders like Switzerland grew bankers, Italy grew designers, and Britain grew writers. Arbor made a campaign promise to build a new trading facility, a commitment to the people on the trading floor.

The financial trade was bigger than the grain trade. But the grain men still had most of the votes and political sway. They made Arbor chairman in 1992.

Arbor backed the electronic trading system still being developed with the Merc, although that system didn't seem to be going anywhere fast. It was bogged down by delays and by political battles. In April 1994, Arbor pulled out of the joint venture. At the Board of Trade, Harold Lavender became the chairman of the exchange's technology committee and dedicated his efforts to developing a handheld computer to be used in the trading pit, a computer to help brokers, not replace them. The future of electronic trading in Chicago looked dubious.

But interest in electronic trading had been sparked somewhere else—in Switzerland. Switzerland was known for cheese, the Alps, and of course secretive banking laws. Charlie Andrews ended up in Switzerland at a meeting sometime in 1989, something he failed to mention in a lawsuit against a client of his, and that meeting became a point that got him thrown in jail in 1995.

In Switzerland, a group of bankers wanted to get into the futures and options business. The Swiss contingent had traveled to Chicago to see its famous trading floors, the exciting mass of people that had drawn visitors for a century, from tourists at the World's Columbian Exposition to politicians to movie stars, including Paul Newman and Robert Redford, who stopped by while shooting a movie in town. People from around the world came to the floors, went home, and built and reworked futures exchanges modeled on those in Chicago. They did that in London, Singapore, and Australia. Most people who came were awed by the excitement and madness. But the Swiss bankers looked at the floors and saw something else—inefficiency. They saw thousands of people running, yelling, trading, and doing the jobs that computers could do.

Back in Switzerland, they set up near Zurich, another financial center on a river and a lake, but with lower buildings, lighter industry, and exacting and efficient people. The Swiss bankers brought in a finance professor who knew about derivatives, and they hired a mathematician as well as some people working at a Chicago consulting firm. They spent two years designing an exchange that would be totally electronic. A computer matched up buyers and sellers. The futures exchange in Australia designed an electronic trading system first, in the wake of the 1987 crash. But the Swiss exchange was completely electronic from the start, with no trading floor at all. They turned on the system in 1989.

Shortly after the Swiss bankers launched, a group of German bankers got together and formed a similar exchange in Frankfurt. They licensed the Swiss bankers' trading system and also launched an all-electronic exchange. They set up some trading terminals in the Netherlands, London, Paris, and even Chicago and recruited people to trade the market electronically. They offered remote membership, so members in London and elsewhere received full and equal electronic access.

The chief executive of the German exchange set up a meeting with Patrick Arbor in Chicago and suggested they work together. Arbor brought that message to the board of directors, who scoffed. They had the biggest futures exchange in the world, with the longest history and the biggest markets. They weren't about to partner with an upstart.

But in 1997 the Germans performed an experiment. They had their computer system do battle with a trading pit, to see what customers would choose. They did that by offering trading on the German bund, the ten-year bond issued by the German government. It was trading in a pit in London. Hundreds of people in colored trading jackets screamed and jostled, packing—or "ramming," as they said in London—into the biggest pit at London's financial futures exchange.

At first, the computer seemed to lose. Overwhelmingly, customers continued trading in the pit. But the German exchange introduced some incentive programs that made it cheaper to trade on the computer. Some people started trading that way, then more. A few months later, traders on the floor in London could tell something was changing. They had less business. They started to leave. Soon the pit was empty, an open wound on the trading floor. In the first real battle of computer versus floor trader, the computer won.

That got noticed in Chicago. The Merc had just taken a step toward computer trading because the Chicago Board of Trade had finally struck a deal to open a futures contract on the Dow Jones industrial average. It seemed like it would be a hit with retail traders, who opened their newspapers in the morning and took note of the Dow. At the Merc, the directors worried it was the death knell for their own stock index futures pit, so out of fear they offered a smaller, all-electronic version of their "spoos" contract. Traders and brokers in the pits paid little attention to it, but it was an immediate hit with customers.

But traders at the Chicago Board of Trade, still the world's largest exchange, were settling into their brand-new trading floor. It was sixty thousand square feet, big enough to house a Boeing 747 if a pilot had decided to park one in the Loop. People fought over position on the floor. In the bond pit, Tom Baldwin complained about his location. Men at the booths surrounding the pits complained they couldn't see well enough into the pits. Some traders on the floor complained that they could see too well. The trading floor was supposed to fix issues of overcrowding, but problems remained, and Arbor warmed to electronic trading. "How quickly it all can change," Arbor said at the Board's annual meeting in February 1998.

And how quickly it did. The Swiss and German exchanges merged into an exchange called Eurex. In March 1998, Arbor signed a letter of intent to work with them to develop a computer system. That December, Arbor, the Board's longest-serving chairman, was ousted after six years on the job, and it was the last time the Chicago Board of Trade could call itself the largest futures exchange in the world.

Carbon   +0.15

In 1998 the directors at the Merc were contemplating the future, and it didn't look good. Floor traders in Europe were losing their war with computers. Older exchanges, including the Merc, looked like they could be dead. The price of a membership was in free-fall.

In the boardroom, Sandner played the role of longtime chairman and statesman. When Sandner stepped down that year, forced out by term limits, he was made "special" policy adviser and given a $200,000 annual salary. Melamed, back from his alleged retirement, played the role of visionary. As "senior" policy adviser, he also received $200,000 a year. The board of directors elected a new chairman, a longtime board member named Scott Gordon, forty-five years old, who had been an executive at several clearing firms, including Melamed's. In the spring of 1998, Gordon stood in front of members during a meeting on the trading floor and announced they would come up with a plan to save the exchange. A member raised his hand and asked them to do it quickly or they'd all be goners.

The exchange was run like a utility and about to topple under its own politics. Its thirty-nine directors met twice a month. It had two hundred committees and three thousand meddling members. They included egg men, hog farmers, cowboys, currency brokers, stockbrokers, Wall Street executives, and brokers catering to retail traders. The directors saw through the crowd and realized they had a business. They came up with a plan to turn their nonprofit club into a for-profit company. That would give them the incentive and money to compete in the midst of the biggest upending of the exchange world in a century.

That appealed to the members, who fell into three groups. One group ran brokerage and clearing firms. Some of those were Chicago firms started by members, but many were well-known Wall Street firms, because as the risk of doing business grew many smaller companies sold to larger ones. Leo Melamed sold his company, Dellsher, to a Japanese bank. Another group included people who remained floor traders. And the final group included people who had their seats but no longer traded on the floor. Many of those members had spent decades building the exchange. As they neared retirement, they were ready to cash out.

The usual way for them to make money on what they had built was to sell their memberships. Or they could "demutualize"—transform the exchange into a for-profit company. A meat trader, Jack Schulte, said this was the opportunity of a lifetime. He spent a year trading at the futures exchange in Sydney, Australia. That small exchange had demutualized and skyrocketed in value.

They spent two years working through the details. The big issue was the trading floor. Some traders were moving "upstairs" to trade on computers. Some clicked keyboards, others wrote code to operate with even less human intervention. This was the dawn of high-frequency trading. But traders on the floor wanted to control their destiny and be able to vote on the issue of computers and the pits. They had enough votes to block any plan, so they won a compromise. The directors would have the right to list any market electronically, but they wouldn't close a pit unless it lost a drastic amount of volume.

In 2000 the board hired James J. McNulty to be chief executive. McNulty had in the 1990s been a partner at O'Connor & Associates, the trading firm the O'Connor brothers started, then had gone on to become an investment banker at Swiss Bank Corporation, which bought the firm. For his expertise, the Merc offered to pay him handsomely—$2 million to join, $1 million in salary, and options to buy up to 5 percent of the exchange's stock if they could demutualize and become publicly traded. They demutualized in November 2000. Then McNulty set about introducing various proposals to professionalize the exchange and get it ready for life as a corporation. He pushed big things, like increasing fees, income, and electronic trading. He also took on the culture. He wanted to establish a brand and said the company's name should be pronounced "Mercan-tyle" rather than "Mercan-till" or "Mercan-teal," which stuck in the craw of some directors. He recommended investment bankers to take the exchange public, and he went on a road show to meet with potential investors, who generally gave polite but blank looks when they heard the name of the company, Chicago Mercantile Exchange. For all that the members had accomplished, some still thought the Merc was the Merchandise Mart, the giant retail building on the Chicago River.

Although McNulty was now the chief executive of a for-profit company, he was still constantly shadowed by Merc members, mainly Melamed and Sandner. They and others on the board chafed at having professional managers take power, especially managers from outside the club. McNulty had a contract. Gordon did not. And Gordon's vice chairman, Terrence "Terry" Duffy, a politically ambitious hog broker, was waiting in the wings. By the time Gordon proposed dropping the generous stipends Melamed and Sandner received, his fate had already been sealed. He was tossed and replaced with Duffy.

On December 6, 2002, the Merc went public. The full members received eighteen thousand shares each. For a few months, the price of a share hovered around $43, making a seat worth roughly $775,000, what Andrews had sold his for in 1995. Then the stock price started to rise. It hit $50 in April, $60 in May, $70 in June, and $100 the following April. Full members who held on to their stock started watching the exchange stock price more than they watched the price of bellies or cattle.

For members who owned multiple seats, like Jack Sandner did, the seats turned out to be the best trades they ever made. As the stock price continued to rise, the Merc's new millionaires bought themselves toys. They bought Bentleys and homes and yachts and condos in Florida. For McNulty, it was a windfall. Other executives did well too.

Others watched in disbelief. Melamed owned just one full seat when the exchange went public. He had poured years of his life into the exchange. When others, including his close friends, were making millions of dollars, he was politicking, pushing the traders into new markets, and relentlessly promoting the exchange. He ended up with more money than most Americans had, but far less money than people around him had. For his service he had political power, lots of glory to feed his ego, and plenty of material for his memoirs. And that, at the end of the day, was what he had. His father would have been proud. Melamed became someone who could say he acted for the greater good.

For a while after the Merc members sold their company, it seemed like nothing had changed. The directors now had to act on behalf of shareholders, but the old members were the new shareholders. When McNulty's contract was up in 2004, the board didn't renew it and replaced him with Craig Donohue, a onetime exchange lawyer who had risen to second-in-command behind McNulty. But however much some may have tried to keep the exchange the same, very quickly it was all different.

The one thing that could change life in Chicago's futures world was computer trading. That was what the European exchanges forced on Chicago in 2004 in a twin corporate attack. The Swiss-German exchange, Eurex, was now the biggest futures exchange in the world. Its all-electronic model had proven to be a winner. People could trade from anywhere in the world, not having to deal with a dirty, smelly, sometimes violent trading pit. A contingent of people set up and traded from Gibraltar, a scenic peninsula sticking out into the Mediterranean Sea. Eurex had seemingly unlimited growth.

The futures traders in London at the London International Financial Futures Exchange, or Liffe for short, had realized the implications of the rise of Eurex. After looking at the empty pit where their loudest traders used to be, the remaining members worked up their own computer system. They combined with a pan-European exchange and went looking for weaker competitors. They put in their scope the Eurodollar traders on the floor of the Merc. The business of trading dollars kept in London banks was, after all, something that it made perfect sense to trade in London.

The Eurodollar pit was barely a pit anymore. It was a stadium. It was giant and full of some of the exchange's toughest and most successful traders. Among the biggest local traders was Leslie Henner Burns, daughter of Bill Henner, who died that year at age eighty. Burns was tough, fair, and a former member of the board of directors. The pit also had members of broker groups, who were particularly powerful there. The Eurodollar market involved huge amounts of money but moved slowly, which gave a broker time to think about who he wanted to trade with and a way to favor certain traders over others. Many of the Eurodollar pit brokers had been confident that they would be able to beat any competition, even from a computer. When facing competition, however, some grew nervous.

The directors of the exchange were panicked. Electronic trading, they could see, was very popular and a real threat. If Liffe turned on a computer, it could suck away all the Eurodollar business overnight, and Eurodollars represented over half the Merc's business. The directors had the right to shut the pit when it lost a certain amount of volume, but by then it would be too late. The brokers and traders on the floor would be left with nothing.

After trading one day, the board of directors held a tense meeting with the Eurodollar pit traders. The chairmen, former and current, all spoke. The goal was to convince the traders to accept an electronic trading ultimatum. Unless one-quarter of the most active volume went digital within three months, the board would be forced to shut down sections of the Eurodollar pit.

Duffy was torn. He came from the trading floor, taken into that family when a trader discovered him pouring beer and gin for traders at a bar near Lake Geneva, Wisconsin. Then Vince

Schreiber from the hog pit gave him a job as a clerk. Duffy bought a seat in 1984, with help from a $50,000 mortgage his parents took out on their home. He became a floor broker and stood for years on the top stair of the pit in an exchange-issued red trading jacket. He developed a reputation as a snappy dresser and an excellent politician.

The meeting was almost as tense as trading in a pit. A close friend of Duffy's argued that the traders had nothing to worry about. A trader stood up and said that he had worked in New York and that bankers would continue sending in orders because they relied on floor traders for information. Applause broke out after some fiery speeches. When Duffy tried to explain that computer trading would change the market, more traders rose to protest.

In the end, the board won its right. And quickly the computer took over. Within a few months, Eurodollar trading migrated to the computer. And floor traders were left stunned.

Down the street, the Board of Trade was also under attack and less able to fight back. The members there owned neither an electronic trading system nor a clearinghouse. The German exchange had been a partner but became an enemy after the deal got expensive and Board of Trade members around the building complained that the "Germans" were taking over. The Board's directors looked at alternatives and voted to use Liffe's electronic trading system instead.

When the Board licensed the system from London, the German exchange set up a U.S. unit in the Sears Tower and prepared to compete with the Board's biggest market, the bond futures contract. What's more, it went to the Board's clearinghouse, a separate entity that for decades had been considered the central bank of the Chicago Board of Trade. Over the years, Wall Street firms had regularly been outvoted at the exchange by floor traders, but the firms gained more power at the clearinghouse. They were happy to give floor traders some competition and struck a deal to clear trades for Eurex too. That would make it easy for large firms to move their trading from the Board of Trade to Eurex.

For longtime members, it was the ultimate insult. The clearing-house was created to keep order at the Board of Trade, but now it had gone rogue. The man in the chairman's seat was forty-nine-year-old Charles Carey. He was a third-generation exchange member whose grandfather Peter had been president and whose uncle Bernie had been chairman. For Carey, a South Side Irishman, it was a family business. He was in a tough spot. There was one way out.

Many chairmen over the years had discussed merging the two exchanges. It made perfect business sense. If the Board of Trade and the Mercantile Exchange merged, they could cut millions of dollars in overhead costs and offer grain, meat, and financial futures in one place. They would have the majority of futures trading in the United States. But the members were not interested. They were antithetical companies, like rival Chicago gangs. They had different bars, different hand signals, and different products. It was like discussing merging the North Side Cubs and the South Side White Sox.

But in January 2003, at a dinner in Boca Raton, Florida, Carey, stogie in mouth, approached Duffy. Carey and Duffy knew each other. When times got slow at the Board in 1983, Carey went to the Merc on and off for four years and traded hogs, where Duffy hung out. They had common backgrounds. Both were South Side Irish, from Democratic families. Carey's grandfather had been Cook County sheriff and a delegate to the 1932 presidential convention. Duffy's grandfather John had been an alderman and Cook County board president, a leader of the area's Democratic machine. Carey told Duffy that he wanted to make a deal for the Board's traders to clear trades through the Merc's clearinghouse. Some members considered it heresy to make a deal with the Merc, long the smaller, less respectable exchange, but it was either that or die or lose to the Europeans.

Back in Chicago, joined by their respective chief executives, they haggled over price at Sullivan's steak house. In April 2003, they signed a deal in which the Merc would clear Board of Trade trades. When Eurex attacked, Carey and his board temporarily dropped some trading prices to zero. Eurex's American exchange filed an antitrust suit, but trading remained at the Board of Trade.

The next step was obvious. In 2005, a few months before the Board of Trade went public, the Merc, chaired by Duffy, made an unsolicited offer to buy the Board of Trade. Carey and his board rejected the offer, at first. But after going public, in October 2005, they had a better idea of what their company was worth. Nine months later, when investors valued the Board of Trade at $6 billion, Carey told Duffy that he was open to a merger.

The next morning Carey and his cousin Peter Carey, a lawyer, showed up at Duffy's house. Donohue brought bagels and lox. The Merc's longtime lawyer appeared too. Duffy made five pots of coffee. Without discussing price, they decided that Duffy would be chairman and that the Merc's trading floors would move into the Board's Art Deco building on La Salle Street. They decided that the company would take the name CME Group. In October 2006, they announced an $8-billion deal.

Their hatchet half-buried, they took on their shared rival: the financial establishment in New York. The Futures Industry Association, a collection of futures brokers like banks and investment houses, complained that the proposed CME Group could have too much power. The Department of Justice opened an inquiry. Duffy and Donohue argued that the two exchanges rarely competed directly and that their chief competition wasn't other futures markets but those vastly larger markets in what were now called over-the-counter derivatives, the swaps market. They figured the trustbusters would back off. The exchanges held an engagement party at the industry's March conference in Boca Raton. Duffy and Carey celebrated until 3:00 AM.

At 6:00 AM the next morning, Carey, shaving and still in his robe, answered a knock at his hotel room and was handed an envelope that he assumed was a party invitation. It turned out to be a counteroffer from the IntercontinentalExchange, a six-year-old Atlanta upstart, which had just finished buying the New York Board of Trade, the exchange that had rolled together the futures markets for coffee, cotton, sugar, and cocoa. Carey called his cousin Peter, who called in lawyers, who instructed Carey to stay put. They reminded him that he had a fiduciary duty. Within those bounds, he made a courtesy call to Duffy to cancel their golf game for later that day.

The Intercontinental was led by Jeffrey Sprecher, who had developed power plants in California and then bought an Atlanta company and built it into an exchange where utilities, oil companies, and banks traded swaps on electricity, natural gas, and crude oil. In 2001 he got into the futures business when he bought London's International Petroleum Exchange, a competitor to the New York Mercantile. While swaps traders didn't need to follow rules that applied to the futures business, he made a business of introducing clearinghouses to them anyway. He made news when he shut the International Petroleum Exchange's trading floor in 2005 and took that exchange all-electronic. The next year he offered the New York Merc's crude oil contract electronically and captured a portion of that business. The New York Merc's members subsequently adopted Globex and moved a lot of trading to the screen.

Both Duffy and Sprecher offered stock for the Board of Trade, but Sprecher offered $1 billion more. He also told analysts that he had "firsthand knowledge" that regulators were "looking carefully" at the terms of the merger.

The Merc guys hurried back to Chicago and held a meeting for the Board of Trade shareholders at the W Hotel. Duffy started with a brief, emotional outburst about his Chicago roots—and said that buying a condo in town couldn't buy Sprecher citizenship to the city. Then, piece by piece, Donohue tore apart the Intercontinental's offer. He argued that the Merc's currency had been proven while Sprecher's looked like an investor fad. But in the Q&A session, member after member demanded that the Merc pay more.

Sandner was playing golf one afternoon when a Board of Trade member approached and prodded him to get the Merc to up its offer. Sandner shooed him off. Duffy got similar pitches daily, over the phone at work, at home, even at his kid's school. Someone buttonholed Donohue at a mall while he was being fitted for a suit. The Merc raised its offer in May, then raised it once more to $11 billion. On Monday, July 9, 2007, the final vote was tallied on the second floor of the Union League Club, a block from the Board of Trade. In the end, 95 percent of the votes backed the deal. They buried the hatchet. The two exchanges, long rivals, became one.

It was, after all, just business now, a corporate deal. Around the world, exchanges that had been member-run institutions went public and merged. That December, in the midst of the consolidation, CME Group's stock topped $700 a share. Some members sold stock and took profits. But like Old Hutch from the 1800s, many traders had trouble getting out while they were ahead. In 2008, the stock price tumbled. CME Group still used it to buy the New York Mercantile Exchange. Electronic trading grew and the pits withered. The shareholders of the CME Group owned what was, by some measures, the largest financial exchange in the world.

When the futures exchanges merged and went corporate, markets were entering a new era. In Chicago, the Board of Trade's former economist Richard Sandor was trying to build another market. Just a few steps north of the Board's building, Sandor promoted a market for carbon greenhouse gases, the Chicago Climate Exchange, which he founded in 2003. He wore a plastic green watch and a green tie. When the *New York Times Magazine* came calling in 2006, Sandor called himself a "humble economist" trying to solve global warming. In 2007, *Time* called him a hero of the environment.

Scientists said people around the world needed to reduce carbon dioxide emissions to fight global warming, and Sandor said the best way to do that was with a market. The idea was to treat carbon like wheat or corn, to standardize and trade it. Countries would cap the amount of carbon dioxide that companies could emit and issue tradable permits representing carbon. A coal plant that polluted would buy permits, and loggers who abstained from cutting down a rain forest could sell permits. Europe adopted this "cap and trade" system. Sandor founded an exchange there as he pushed for the United States to adopt a similar system. A commissioner of the Commodity Future Trading Commission in June 2008, speaking at a carbon trading conference, called the potential size of a carbon market "unequivocally vast. It is certainly possible that the emissions markets could overtake all other commodity markets at some point down the road."

But it was hard to make the market work. The underlying premise was that carbon was a commodity that people could measure and trade. But measuring air was not easy. Sandor said his members used independent third parties to keep accurate measurements of the carbon they emitted and offset. But others questioned how much carbon came off of trees, for example, or was absorbed back into the ground. Besides that, he needed a government cap to create demand for carbon permits, and Congress seemed in no hurry to implement a cap. So the carbon market remained immature.

Meanwhile, the markets already in existence were hitting bumps. The futures prices of grains skyrocketed. Around the world, the high prices caused unrest and riots. Pundits and academics debated whether the prices properly reflected supply and demand or were artificially inflated by speculators. And the price of crude oil rose, which became a major political issue in Washington, where House Speaker Nancy Pelosi held a press conference before Independence Day in 2008 and proclaimed, "Oil speculators are making money by betting against American consumers at the pump." News sources constantly reported the price of crude oil on the futures markets, and people trading crude oil futures were under scrutiny. They were the focal point of debate and deemed either messengers or manipulators, although in the background, large trades affecting food and crude oil prices were also being made with swaps.

Meanwhile, there was a bubble brewing in real estate, the same market that had drawn so many speculators to frontier Chicago. Homes, the cornerstones of communities, were the subject of wild trading. Politicians remained attached to a utopian vision and encouraged home buying. Banks lent money freely, barely looking at the borrowers. Although mortgage futures no longer traded at the Chicago Board of Trade, Wall Street still turned mortgages into bonds to be sliced, diced, and sold. Mortgage and real estate brokers encouraged people to borrow money and buy homes quickly.

At the country's largest financial institutions, people perfected new kinds of swaps, namely credit default swaps, which were used to insure mortgage-backed products. And the swaps were used to speculate. Like the original futures, swaps concentrated the surrounding frenzy into a financial instrument, and people traded those with the light supervision that regulators had decided was appropriate for swaps traders.

As real estate prices shot up, so did buildings. In Chicago, developers built tall condominium buildings on all sides of the Loop. Two miles south, on Prairie Avenue, developers put up new homes next to old ones, and they put up multi-story buildings that dwarfed the homes. Steps from the site of the Fort Dearborn Massacre, developers prepared to erect two super-tall, shiny towers, far taller than anything else in the neighborhood. A group of neighbors complained, but plans progressed. The market was now about numbers, not neighbors.

In the 1970s, Thomas Bomar, the chief executive of Freddie Mac, had fretted that pools of mortgages could lose value. Three decades later, in the frenzied market, they did. Teaser mortgage rates expired. Homeowners saw their mortgage bills jump, and some couldn't pay. One thing led to the next, and the market crumbled. The housing market collapsed. Some banks that had made loans collapsed. Some companies that had used swaps to provide insurance on mortgages collapsed, or nearly did. The financial system itself came close to collapse. Taxpayers stepped in, rescued institutions, and paid off swaps trades to keep the financial markets functioning.

Loans dried up, and the economy tipped into recession. Brokers found other work. Developers who did shoddy work dissolved their companies. Homeowners defaulted and walked away from mortgages. The towers planned for Prairie Avenue were not built.

The year looked like a referendum on free markets and on capitalism itself. But there was a better test case—the futures markets, which was still understood or appreciated only by a few. They had even confounded the theorists. Merton Miller, one of the University of Chicago's Nobel Prize–winning economists, had been a director of both the Board of Trade and the Merc. He at times looked at Chicago's overcrowded pits and suggested that the exchanges auction off the real estate and give the best spots to the highest bidders. The traders shrugged him off. They had their own rules of order.

The futures business had been a laboratory and harbinger. It was built by people who turned grain trading into what seemed the wildest business on earth. But while futures looked at times like capitalism unleashed, in reality the business balanced individual freedoms with an unlikely social responsibility. Futures traders were selfish in the pits, but they ran their exchanges as clubs, and they submitted to occasional government intervention. Academics had their own thoughts about free markets, but those thoughts at times made a caricature of capitalism. Futures traders were imperfect and practical, wild to a point. Theory aside, they ran real free markets.

The people in the pits ran their markets for decades. But as the money involved grew, the futures markets morphed and changed, and the exchanges evolved, as societies do. Individuals were dwarfed by institutions. Brokers were replaced by people who traded from their home computers with software, not people, tracking their trades. Traders were replaced altogether by computers running algorithms.

The futures markets will never be replicated again as they existed, nor need they be. They left blueprints showing how a group of people constructed markets that, on balance, worked well. The markets were based on real things exchanged by real people, who were as greedy as anyone but used their own money and their own names. No matter how complex finance becomes, having a community of people who have to live with their decisions and each other at the end of each day is a simple tonic for many ills.

|. . .|

To be sure, the futures markets had its problems. The opportunities attracted gamblers, manipulators and scam artists, and the merely misguided. The people causing problems were often labeled speculators, a word with so much baggage that it should be sent on permanent vacation. "Speculator" is now used interchangeably with "profiteer."

But the word "speculator" predates the futures business. It comes from Latin and a word that means "spy" or "scout." *Merriam-Webster's Dictionary* says it means to "meditate or ponder a subject" or "to assume a business risk in hope of gain." By that definition, tailors speculate when they buy fabric they hope to sell in the form of a suit. Truckers speculate when they drive long hauls and hope to be paid at the end. And farmers speculate when they buy seeds and fertilizer that they hope to turn into crops and sell for a profit. Everyone with an entrepreneurial spirit is a speculator.

We need them, as did Chicago. In 1871 the city of Chicago went up in flames. The *Chicago Tribune* editor Joseph Medill remained optimistic. "Looking upon the ashes of thirty years' accumulations, the people of this once beautiful city have resolved that Chicago shall rise again," he wrote. He was only one of the people who looked at burned-out, flat prairie land and bet it would recover. People built railroads, airports, and skyscrapers. They built local government, famous for corruption, and food companies and retail giants. They rebuilt the futures exchange. Medill could have been wrong or changed his mind at any point. But luckily, his first instinct was right, and Chicago rose.

EPILOGUE
The Future

On that cold day in January, Charlie Andrews finishes eating his sole sandwich. He says he and a few other men from the Kansas City stockyards brought the idea of cattle futures to the people at the Chicago Merc back in the early 1960s, which would mean that much of the innovation started with him. That is one version of the story. He leaves early that afternoon, trying to stay ahead of a snowstorm, to make cattle deals in a few states on his way back to his ranch and his home office, where the television plays CNBC. A stock ticker crawls across the bottom of the screen, and a CNBC reporter named Rick Santelli periodically broadcasts from the futures trading floor in Chicago. In February 2009 Santelli went on an on-air rant about accountability and, while cheered on by traders in the background, blasted a plan to use government money to refinance "the losers' mortgages." He invited viewers to a "Chicago tea party" at Lake Michigan, became a media sensation, and sparked a Tea Party political movement.

Andrews leaves the Board of Trade building, where CME Group has consolidated the trading floors, so the Merc and Board of Trade traders who remain are getting to know each other in the newest trading room. It is still a family business. Third- and fourth-generation traders work in the pits. Irish traders with prayer cards in their pockets and a few brothers nearby trade steps from men whose families had businesses on Fulton Street. It is also a melting pot of Chicagoans. A man sells homemade jerky on the floor in a rainbow of flavors. A former Buddhist monk from the border of Tibet works as a runner on the floor. The most active pit is the Standard and Poor's stock index pit, still a small stadium with men jumping, yelling, and gesturing to one another. One man looks a lot like Elvis, and two men are on the verge of a fistfight when others pull them apart. A few retired members still come to the floor every day, just to hang out and be near the action. But as more trading is done electronically, people leave the floor one by one.

As Andrews leaves the building, he walks through the lobby. Above him on the second floor, behind a nondescript door, are the offices of a high-frequency trading firm started by two floor traders. It's one of the biggest trading firms in the financial world.

Andrews exits below the large windows on La Salle Street that overlook the original trading floor. That room has been gutted and turned into another office, a light, open space with people sitting at desks and computers, trading options. Throughout the building, firms and the exchange have run wires and cables to handle high-speed trading.

As he pulls out of the city, he bypasses a few grain elevators. They're still around on the South Side, most unused and only holding up the sky. A local writer describes the elevators as "slowly deteriorating like Egyptian ruins in an urban desert, standing as a final reminder of Chicago's agricultural past." Andrews passes Fulton Street, which still has food businesses and trucks. Mexican workers stand outside on loading docks, smoking. Fulton Market Cold Storage is still there, a large building with cavernous, frozen rooms filled with stacks of boxes. It doesn't keep eggs anymore, however. The few small egg companies nearby, on the street, move eggs in and out quickly, to conform with government regulations.

Most of the cold storage warehouses and other buildings in the area have been turned into loft condominiums. Across the street is a storefront housing an aesthetic dermatologist, another has Tibetan carpets for sale, and another is home to a sculptor. Farther east, one old building is now a fancy restaurant called

Publican, which serves up expensive plates of pork to well-dressed diners sitting at long, communal tables. The dining room is loud; the lights are bare bulbs. People who live on Fulton Street like these new businesses. They like the feeling of the neighborhood, but not the reality of the food businesses that were there before. Neighbors complain about the smells and the late-night noise from trucks arriving and leaving with food. Even though Fulton Street is no longer the food hub that it was, neighbors would like that business to disappear entirely.

That has almost happened to South Water Market, where produce sellers used to work. The twelve-story building that housed many merchants is gone. In its place is a parking lot. The cold storage warehouse nearby is apartments. The low buildings that were full of food stores—where Jack Carl was the apple man—are also condos and townhomes. Former loading docks are now porches, some with tables and potted plants. It's another market lost to the residential real estate boom.

The stockyards are gone, replaced by an industrial park. All that's left is the gate, with the image of a steer, and a sign that the city put up with black and white pictures of what was there. One lone meatpacking plant still operates.

Fort Dearborn is long gone. Markers on the street show where it used to stand. And two miles south, where the early Chicagoans walked on the frontier, and got attacked, there is now a park. Around the corner are a few mansions that still grace Prairie Avenue. They are surrounded by townhomes. Nearby are factories that, when built in the 1900s, sent rich residents fleeing. Some of these factories were converted into loft condominiums in the recent real estate boom. But one, just off Prairie Avenue, is a big brick building with gothic arches and decorative terra cotta shields on the outside. It was solidly built to house very heavy printing presses for a company that printed directories and catalogs. When presses changed, the company vacated and sold the building. Today, law firms and telecommunications companies have moved computers into the empty space. So have trading companies. The windows reveal little. Most neighbors wonder what goes on inside.

Inside, security is tight. Now a visitor needs an escort and identification to get past the lobby, which still has marble floors and high stone ceilings. If you have an escort, take an elevator to another lobby and another security desk, then enter a room where a door behind you has to shut before one in front opens. Then comes a hand scanner. Beyond that are large rooms in semi-darkness, with colored cables running overhead and rows of computers in metal cages, humming. Some of these computers are owned by trading firms, some started by people who traded futures on the trading floors. At least one of the computers is owned by CME Group. The traders' computers send more orders, faster than ever. They run high-frequency trading algorithms that try to beat others to the trade. It's quiet. This data center is the new floor, and one or more of these cages house the new pits.

This room seems the domain of a more elite and anonymous club of traders who use money and expertise to build and ply a super-fast trade. They represent a new group of speculators in the trading community, so there's a new era of market building and evolution ahead.

Andrews drives off and heads back to Kansas. That is and always has been his home. He came to Chicago to trade, but now he can do his job from anywhere, just like other people at home can log onto computers and trade through discount brokers. It has become easier and cheaper to trade. Now that the trading floors are gone, he is happiest closest to his ranch and cattle business. For him the business is still about animals and the people who trade them. It always was.

ACKNOWLEDGMENTS

For the past eighteen months, this book has been an excuse for me to meet an endless line of fascinating people. Each person I interviewed sent me to someone else, and the reporting led from Chicago to Kansas, New York, California, London, Australia, Switzerland, and even to Africa at one point. But it always led back to Chicago.

There are a few people in particular I'd like to thank. The Board of Trade broker henceforth to be known as "Opie" let me hang out and observe the always well-behaved gents of the Dow pit. Buck Haworth, formerly of the Chicago Mercantile Exchange's Eurodollar pit, was always available to offer details, opinions, and context. Glenn Windstrup, master of many trades, helped me see that business was simpler than it seemed. Harold Lavender, the first person I met in the industry, helped demystify what can be very mystifying. Drew Mauck reliably introduced me to people on and around La Salle Street. Ira Zeidman, Steve Errera, Jay Sorkin, Maurie Schneider, Joe Sullivan, and others, some who asked not to be named, donated hours of time. Unfortunately for them, they'll never get those hours back.

My editors and colleagues at *Forbes* put me in the position where I could explore this world. Tim Sullivan, my patient editor at Basic Books, read an article I wrote about Chicago's exchanges and believed there was more to the story. David Fugate, at Launch-Books, helped make it happen.

Every time I stepped into Ceres Café in the Board of Trade building, Billy Assimos there asked if I was done yet. And I wouldn't be if not for the people who helped me gather and mold my thoughts into something more coherent. So thank you to my perpetual professor, Jonathan Friendly; the fellows and staff at the Property and Environment Research Center in Bozeman, Montana; New York's most talented travel writer, David Landsel; smart editor Jason Torres; and my friend and neighbor Kim Le, who generously lent me her apartment.

I developed a new appreciation for the local treasure trove known as the Chicago Public Library, and for librarians. What the public library didn't have, I found—or more accurately was guided to find—in the Chicago History Museum, in newspaper archives, and, through Curt Zuckerman, in the CME Group's "knowledge center," among other places.

Thank you to Dori Byard, who is my guide to farm country, and to my friends and family, especially my mother, Linda Roffe, and husband, Joseph Colitto. You're only reading this because in 2004 he was game to move to the Windy City and have a little adventure. He encouraged me to keep writing during the most inconvenient times possible. So I hope it was worth it.

A NOTE ABOUT
SOURCES

Most of the information in this book comes from interviews with one hundred–plus people who work in or around the futures business. I quickly discovered that everyone remembered episodes differently, and frequently people disagreed with and contradicted each other. I tried to verify stories with documents and multiple people. In addition to that, I gathered information from newspaper clippings, especially from the online archives of the *Chicago Tribune*, and I relied on the following written books and journals.

Cronon, William. *Nature's Metropolis: Chicago and the Great West.* New York: W. W. Norton, 1991.

Dies, Edward Jerome. *The Plunger: A Tale of the Wheat Pit.* New York: Covici-Friede, 1929.

Falloon, William D. *Market Maker: A Sesquicentennial Look at the Chicago Board of Trade.* Chicago: Board of Trade of the City of Chicago, 1998.

Grossman, James R., Ann Durkin Keating, and Janice L. Reiff. *The Encyclopedia of Chicago.* Chicago: University of Chicago Press, 2004.

Helm, Linai Taliaferro, and Nelly Kinzie Gordon. *The Fort Dearborn Massacre.* Chicago: Rand-McNally, 1912.

Hieronymus, Thomas Applegate. *Economics of Futures Trading, for Commercial and Personal Profit.* New York: Commodity Research Bureau, 1971.

Keegan, Edward. *The Chicago Board of Trade Building: A Building Book from the Chicago Architecture Foundation.* San Francisco: Pomegranate, 2005.

Liebling, A. J. *Chicago: The Second City.* Lincoln: University of Nebraska Press, 2004.

Magrath, C. Peter. "A Foot in the Door." *American Heritage* (February 1964).

McKenzie, Donald. "Constructing a Market, Performing Theory: The Historical Sociology of a Financial Derivatives Exchange." *American Journal of Sociology* (2003).

Melamed, Leo, and Bob Tamarkin. *Leo Melamed: Escape to the Futures*. New York: John Wiley & Sons, 1996.

Miller, Donald L. *City of the Century: The Epic of Chicago and the Making of America*. New York: Simon & Schuster, 1996.

Miller, Norman C. *The Great Salad Oil Swindle*. New York: Coward McCann, 1965.

Norris, Frank. *The Pit: A Story of Chicago*. New York: Doubleday, Page, 1903.

Rodengen, Jeffrey L., Ann Gossy, Ryan Milewicz, and Richard M. Daley. *Past, Present, and Futures: Chicago Mercantile Exchange*. Fort Lauderdale, Fla.: Write Stuff Enterprises, 2008.

Tamarkin, Bob. *The Merc: The Emergence of a Global Financial Powerhouse*. New York: HarperBusiness, 1993.

Tyre, William H. *Chicago's Historic Prairie Avenue*. Charleston, S.C.: Arcadia Publishing, 2008.

INDEX